The Open University

Business School

Unit 7

Business law and finance

Written by Jane Frecknall-Hughes

Module Team

Dr Devendra Kodwani, *B291 Chair & Author*
Dr Carien van Mourik, *Author*
Professor Jane Frecknall-Hughes, *Professional Certificate in Accounting Chair & Author*
Catherine Gowthorpe, *Author*
Kelly Dobbs, *Curriculum Assistant*
Elizabeth R Porter, *Regional Manager*
Sam Cooper, *Programme Coordinator*
Emir Forken, *Qualifications Manager*
Dr Lesley Messer, *Programme Manager*
Funmi Mapelujo, *Curriculum Manager*

External Assessor

Professor Stuart Turley, Manchester Business School

Critical Readers

Professor Judy Day, Manchester Business School
Elizabeth R Porter
Professor Peter Walton

Developmental Testers

Dr Teodora Burnand
Sam Cooper
Vimal Goricha
Vani Shri Goswami
Dudley Hughes

Production Team

Martin Brazier, *Graphic Designer*
Anne Brown, *Media Assistant*
Sarah Cross, *Print Buyer*
Beccy Dresden, *Media Project Manager*
Vicky Eves, *Graphic Artist*
Paul Hoffman, *Editor*
Diane Hopwood, *Rights Assistant*
Lucinda Simpson, *Editor*
Kelvin Street, *Library*
Ryan Rushton, *Learning Media Developer*
Liz McCarthy-Williams, *Media Project Manager*

Software

Accounting package software was designed by and remains the property of Sage plc.

Other Material

The Module Team wishes to acknowledge use of some material from B680 *The Certificate in Accounting*.

This publication forms part of the Open University module B291 *Financial accounting*. Details of this and other Open University modules can be obtained from the Student Registration and Enquiry Service, The Open University, PO Box 197, Milton Keynes MK7 6BJ, United Kingdom (tel. +44 (0)845 300 60 90; email general-enquiries@open.ac.uk).

Alternatively, you may visit the Open University website at www.open.ac.uk where you can learn more about the wide range of modules and packs offered at all levels by The Open University.

To purchase a selection of Open University materials visit www.ouw.co.uk, or contact Open University Worldwide, Walton Hall, Milton Keynes MK7 6AA, United Kingdom for a brochure (tel. +44 (0)1908 858793; fax +44 (0)1908 858787; email ouw-customer-services@open.ac.uk).

The Open University

Walton Hall

Milton Keynes

MK7 6AA

First published 2010. Third edition 2015.

Edited and designed by The Open University.

Typeset in India by OKS Prepress Services, Chennai.

Printed in the United Kingdom by Henry Ling Limited, at the Dorset Press, Dorchester, DT1 1HD

ISBN 978 1 4730 0207 4

3.1

Contents

Introduction

Welcome to Unit 7. This is the final unit of B291 and it focuses on law, business administration and finance, and their relevance in the context of an accountant's work. You have already encountered some aspects of law in earlier units. For instance, you learned in Unit 1 that there are different legal forms which firms may use to carry on their business activities and that such differences in legal form may give rise to different accounting treatment, format and disclosure in financial statements. You have especially seen in Unit 5 how some of the regulations affect partnerships and companies in terms of their financial statements, and, to some extent, how they are permitted to raise finance.

In Units 1 and 5 we have referred to the *Partnership Act 1890*,[1] the *Limited Partnerships Act 1907*, the *Limited Liability Partnerships Act 2000* (in England, Wales and Scotland) and the *Limited Liability Partnerships Act (Northern Ireland) 2002* in Northern Ireland, and the *Companies Act 2006*. However, these Acts form part of a much wider body of laws governing society as a whole, some of which regulate particularly the environment in which businesses operate, such as the rules governing how businesses make deals or how they must treat employees. Accountants need to understand such things as they are often faced with the task of accounting for their financial effects. Unit 7 will consider this wider legal environment.

The law topics considered in Unit 7 comprise areas of study in their own right, and are extensive. We provide here only an introduction to the business-related aspects, but there are many legal textbooks that can provide more in-depth reading if you wish to read more about any of the topics covered in this unit. If you do consult other material, please make sure that you have the most up to date version of any text, as law, like accounting, is an area subject to rapid and often extensive changes. A suggested list of useful textbooks for further reading is included at the end of the unit, but this is by no means exhaustive.

Unit 7 consists of seven main sessions and, since it is the final unit of the B291 module, it will also offer some final thoughts in respect of the module as a whole.

Session 1 outlines the difference between criminal and civil law, the sources of English law (as a common law system), including case law and the doctrine of judicial precedent, and compares and contrasts different legal systems, such as codified (civil law) systems, Sharia Law and international legal regulations.

Session 2 introduces the law of tort, especially the tort of negligence and the essential elements of duty of care, breach of that duty, damage, loss, injury and liability. It considers the relevance of negligence in relation to professional advisers.

Session 3 introduces the law of contract, including the elements of a valid contract and the required forms of contract in specific circumstances. It considers, therefore, matters such as offer and

---

[1] Unless otherwise stated, all Acts of Parliament referred to are those of the UK Parliament.

acceptance, contractual capacity, consideration, intention to create legal relations, an absence of vitiating factors and matters related to performance and non-performance. For most contracts these things are straightforward, but you will see that many problems can arise when all these elements are not incontrovertibly present.

Session 4 deals with the law of employment. It explains how 'employees' differ from 'self-employed persons', and the essential elements of a contract of employment; the difference between 'unfair' and 'wrongful' dismissal; and the impact on employers and employees of health and safety legislation and the various pieces of anti-discrimination legislation.

Session 5 introduces the law of agency. It defines what is meant by the terms 'agent' and 'principal', explains how an agency relationship is established and helps you to understand the concept of authority, and the possible liabilities of both agent and principal.

Session 6 turns to considering issues associated with company form and formation, such as the implications of corporate personality, 'corporate veil' (and when this may be lifted) and the corporate capacity to contract. It deals with the procedure for registering a company, the advantages of purchasing a company 'off the shelf', and the purpose, legal status and contents of the Memorandum and Articles of Association and other company documents, such as the statutory books.

Session 7 goes on to consider further aspects of company administration and finance. It deals with basic concepts and principles underlying company administration (with reference to directors, shareholders and the company secretary), and finance (in terms of share and loan capital, especially debentures).

After Session 7 and the summary for Unit 7, there is a summary for the whole module.

Learning aims and outcomes of Unit 7

Upon completion of Unit 7 you are expected to be able to understand and explain:

1   the basic differences between English and other legal systems
2   the basic principles underlying the laws of tort, contract, agency and employment
3   legal matters associated with the company form, especially in terms of the formation of companies
4   the concepts and principles underlying company administration and finance.

> **Activity timings**
>
> Please note that, unless advised otherwise, you should expect to spend no more than 15–20 minutes on the activities in this unit.

If you wish to read further details of any of the cases cited in this unit, this can be done by logging on to the Westlaw or LexisLibrary legal databases which are available via The Open University Library website. All you need to do is click on the 'cases' tab, and type in at least one of the names of the parties given in the case name.

You will see that case law material in Unit 7 is used in various ways. Sometimes a case will be discussed in detail, with many of the facts being given, as facts will be fundamental to the development of a particular legal issue. At other times, you may just see a case name being given. This latter does not necessarily imply that the case is less important, but often means that the facts (often straightforward) confirm a general point made in the text. Where cases have been discussed in detail, you will find it useful to memorise the basic facts and decisions as knowledge of these can often be used to enhance your answers to examination questions. For example, you will not be able to answer any question on the development of financial negligence without knowing the case law referred to in Section 2.4 or answer a question about contract law without knowing the case law discussed in Section 3.2.4. These are the types of cases to know in detail as they are instrumental to the development of the law in a particular area. However, you should try to remember as many other cases as possible.

While it is helpful to know and cite the name of the case and the date, credit will be given for being able to repeat details of the case and judgment, even if the exact case name and date cannot be remembered.

You will also find a lot of new terms used in this unit. Unfortunately, even in a unit which is just an introduction to the subject of law, it is necessary to use the terminology which is both correct and usual for the subject, so this is unavoidable. However, the more you study the text and refer to the online glossary, the more familiar you will become with these forms of expression.

SESSION **1** # The basic differences between English and other legal systems

Introduction

Upon completion of Session 1 you are expected to be able to:

- understand the difference between criminal and civil law
- identify and explain the sources of English law (as a common law system), including case law and the doctrine of judicial precedent
- compare and contrast different legal systems, such as codified (civil law) systems, Sharia Law and international legal regulations.

Session 1 helps you understand the legal background in which business in general operates and the differences in legal systems between different jurisdictions.

1.1 The difference between criminal and civil law

If there were no enforceable laws, society would be dysfunctional and anarchic, and people would be able to do whatever they wanted without fear of hindrance or punishment. Laws are required to determine acceptable standards in terms of how individuals, companies, etc., behave and to set punishments for those who breach those standards. In most modern societies there are two main categories of legal rules – criminal law and civil law – which are discussed below.

1.1.1 Criminal law

A crime is regarded as an offence against the laws of an ordered society as a whole, and the state, on behalf of society, takes action to punish the offender(s). It is because the state takes action here, not particular individuals, that criminal law falls within the body of law known as Public Law.

Public Law includes **constitutional law**, **administrative law** *and* **tax law** *as well as criminal law. It is the part of the law which deals with the relationship between individuals and the state, and relationships between individuals that are of direct concern to the state. It deals with the constitution and functions of the different organs of central and local government.*

The purpose of criminal law is to set rules to govern behaviour in society enabling people to live together harmoniously, by outlawing certain kinds of behaviour, such as murder, various forms of violence against individuals, theft, fraud, etc. Transgressors are punished both as a form of retribution and to deter others from similar acts. This was one of the reasons that punishments in the past were often carried out in public, for example, public hangings as punishment for murder.

1.1.2 Civil law

Private Law deals with aspects of relationships between individuals that are of no direct concern to the state. It includes the **law of property**, *the* **law of trusts**, **family law**, *the* **law of contract**, *the* **law of tort** *and* **mercantile law**.

The purpose of civil law is to enable disagreements between citizens to be resolved in a peaceful manner. It works in a way that complements criminal law, but defines the rights and duties of citizens between themselves, rather than between the state and citizens. Because in civil law actions are between private individuals or bodies, civil law falls within the body of law known as Private Law.

In civil law, if an individual breaches another's rights, the wronged person can claim compensation from the wrongdoer, which is referred to as damages and usually takes the form of a monetary award. Thus civil law also regulates behaviour in society, although in a different way from criminal law. If people know that they may be called upon to pay in some way for a breach of another's rights, then they may think carefully before acting in such a way.

1.1.3   Criminal and civil law compared

In most countries, the criminal and civil courts are separate, and different terminology is used to describe what happens. The table below gives an example of the different proceedings in England and Wales.

Table 1   Difference in criminal and civil proceedings in England and Wales

	Criminal prosecution	*Civil action*
Institutor of proceedings	The state	An individual (the claimant, formerly referred to as the plaintiff)
Term to describe the prosecution/action	Prosecutes	Sues
Term to describe party prosecuted/against whom action is taken	Accused	Defendant
Purpose of proceedings	To punish the accused	To obtain a legal remedy* from the defendant
Outcome if prosecution/ action is successful	Imprisonment or fine to the appropriate authority	Usually damages payable to the claimant

* A remedy (sometimes also referred to as a redress or relief, and sometimes preceded by the word 'legal') is any of the methods permitted by law to protect or recover rights or obtain redress for their infringement. In civil cases, remedies are commonly damages, but as you will learn later, other remedies may be possible or preferred.

In a criminal case, the state takes action. In England and Wales, this will be taken by the state's prosecution arm in the form of the Crown Prosecution Service. It is not the victim who takes the decision to prosecute. In some cases there may not actually be a direct victim. For example, in the case of an attempted, but unsuccessful theft, nothing might have been stolen, but an offence will still have been committed. In a criminal case, the accused must normally be proved guilty beyond reasonable doubt.

In a civil case, the action is started by the victim (claimant), and the burden of proof is not as great. Liability is usually proved on the balance of probabilities. For the claimant to succeed, it must be demonstrated that his/her case is more probable than the defendant's. Here, hopefully, Activity 1.1 will help you understand how difficult this can be in practice.

'You can plead guilty or not guilty. You cannot plead "Oops!".'

Activity 1.1 ....

Clive owns a bull terrier, Gnasher. Clive falls ill with influenza and asks his friend, Derek, to take Gnasher out for a walk. They go to the local park where Derek lets Gnasher off the lead. Gnasher promptly runs off and disappears from view. Derek hears screams and cries for help, and rounds the corner to see Gnasher fighting with Mrs Evans's poodle, Humphrey.

The *Dangerous Dogs Act 1991, s.3(1)* states:

> If a dog is dangerously out of control in a public place –
>
> (a) the owner; and
>
> (b) if different, the person for the time being in charge of the dog is guilty of an offence, or, if the dog while so out of control injures any person, an aggravated offence, under this sub-section.

Further, *s.1(1)* and *s.2(d)* say that dangerous breeds of dog should be muzzled if in a public place.

Questions

Has an offence been committed?

If so, by whom?

For developing an answer, you may find it helpful to adopt the following process.

- Examine the facts, and decide which are relevant and which are not.
- Identify the relevant law (here given to you, as above).
- Apply the relevant law to the facts.
- Draw conclusions.

Spend about 30–40 minutes developing an answer to these questions.

Feedback

Examining the facts

One way of dealing with this might be to ask the following questions.

1   Did Gnasher (G) attack Mrs Evans (Mrs E)?
2   Did G attack Humphrey (H)?
3   What sort of dog is G?
4   Was G muzzled?
5   Was Derek (D) a fit and proper person to be in charge of G?
6   In whose charge was H?

The information we are given does not provide answers to most of these questions. All we know is that G is a bull terrier, was off the lead and was 'fighting with' H. We do not know if H was in Mrs E's charge, or another person's, or whether H was on a lead or not. All we know is that someone screams (who may or may not be Mrs E, the person in charge of H, or someone passing by). We do not know if a person has been attacked or is screaming for another reason (fright or surprise at the dogs fighting, or something completely unrelated). The fact that G is a bull terrier and H a poodle, may allow the inference that G attacked H, or possibly a person, but this is not in any way certain. G may be a very gentle dog, and H vicious. It is essential that we analyse what we know here. One can often make unwarranted assumptions, for example, that Mrs E is actually present, that she is taking H for a walk and/or that she has been attacked. (Did you make these assumptions yourself?)

We then need to consider what are, and what are not, relevant facts.

Relevant

- Derek (D) is in charge of the dog (G) and therefore liable if there is an offence.
- Clive (C) owns G and is therefore liable if there is an offence (although he has a defence under *s.3(2)* – not given here, but reasonably inferable – if D was a fit and proper person to be in charge of G).
- D has let G off his lead (relevant to whether G was out of control and whether D is fit to be in charge of G).
- D cannot see G, as he has run off and disappeared from view.
- G is fighting with another dog, and *may* have attacked that dog.
- G is a bull terrier – a potentially dangerous breed. (If a pit bull terrier, by *s.1(1)* and *2(d)* it should have been muzzled and kept on a lead.)

Some of these points also apply potentially to Mrs E and whosoever (if anyone) might have been in charge of H.

Irrelevant

- C's dog's name is Gnasher (unless this implies a tendency to bite).
- C has influenza.
- C's friend is called Derek.
- D is walking the dog because C is ill.
- The other dog's name is Humphrey.

Identifying the relevant law and applying it to the facts

One can then develop a checklist for applying the relevant law (here given in the question) to the facts.

- Is D the owner? No.
- Is D 'for the time being in charge of' G? Yes.
- Is G in a public place? Yes.
- Is G 'dangerously out of control'?
  - ⁊ Is G out of control? G is off the lead and D cannot see G, but G might be wearing a muzzle. G might not be out of control at all. H might be the one out of control and could have attacked G.

    ○   Is G dangerous? Would one reasonably believe G would attack another dog or a person? Might the same not be asked about of H?

The first three bullet points apply potentially to Mrs E (or anyone who might be in charge of H) and H.

Drawing conclusions

At this point one might be able to draw tentative conclusions. It is possible that both C and D have committed an offence – but also it is possible that Mrs E (and anyone in charge of H) could have done so, as we know so little about H's position.

There can be an offence even if the dog(s) did not actually injure anyone, if there are reasonable grounds for thinking that this might have happened. As far as we know, it is not an **aggravated offence** because G (and H) did not actually injure anyone.

Activity 1.1 does not involve any aspect of business law, but takes a situation that anyone might encounter in daily life, which is governed by certain rules – here the *Dangerous Dogs Act 1991*. You may have found that you made certain assumptions about the facts which, upon further reflection, were not warranted. After that further reflection, you may find yourself annoyed that you cannot now come to a definite conclusion as to what had happened and who was 'guilty'. This is often the case with a legal problem, as otherwise it would not need to come to a court of law for a decision to be reached. You should find, however, that you have weighed and considered what you do know, and what you do not know, and the various implications of that knowledge, and lack of knowledge, and have come to a more balanced view of the issue, based on your considerations. This is the best way to approach a legal problem – 'if X is the case, then Y will follow; if not, then Z...' and so on. If you have done this, then you have moved forward in developing the way you think, which should be of great assistance to you in approaching legal issues. This said, however, it is still fair to acknowledge that some law is extremely complicated and voluminous and requires experts to deal with it.

'It looks like they're bringing in the new regulations manual.'

Some kinds of events are both a criminal offence and a civil wrong. While a wrongdoer may be fined or imprisoned following conviction for a crime, for example, fraud, the criminal conviction will not necessarily provide the victim of the crime with any remedy, so civil law must be invoked to provide the victim with a means of obtaining compensation (often financial, provided that the wrongdoer has sufficient funds).

1.2 The sources of English law

There are several different sources of English law:

- custom and common law
- equity
- English legislation of various kinds
- European law
- other sources.

These will be discussed below. Different countries have different sources of law and different legal traditions, and these will be discussed in Section 1.3. Many countries have adopted a system based on the English system, so understanding this will help to provide a good conceptual base from which to develop a wider understanding.

1.2.1 Custom and common law

A custom is a practice that has been followed in a particular place in circumstances such that it is to be accepted as part of the law of that place. After the Norman conquest of England in 1066, the Normans attempted to use the body of local customs as a basis of their law, though there were often disputes as to what was and was not customary practice. In order for something to be accepted as a customary law, a formal procedure was introduced: the custom must be reasonable in nature and must have been followed continuously, since the beginning of legal memory.

Legal memory is the period over which the law's recollection extends. The *Statute of Westminster I* of 1275 arbitrarily fixed its commencement at 1189. Time before legal memory is referred to as **time immemorial**, while **living memory** is the period of time over which the recollection of living people extends.

Over time, customs that could be generally applied became common to all areas of the country, and so became common law applicable everywhere. However, this kind of law was not written down in the way, for example, that Acts of Parliament are (see Section 1.2.3), although the cases in which common law was used and applied came to be recorded in formal law reports, so there was a record of decisions taken. The way that common law develops is from case to case, which helps develop principles to meet changing circumstances. For this reason, common law is sometimes referred to as 'case law' or 'judge-made law', although for a long time a fiction was maintained that judges did no more than apply the underlying body of customary rules and usages constituting the common law. In order to ensure certainty, the principles emerging from cases judged in the higher courts are binding on lower courts under the doctrine of judicial precedent (see Section 1.2.6). In England the common law co-exists with a body of specifically written law or legislation, also referred to as codified law (see Section 1.3.2), and with equity, which is discussed in Section 1.2.2.

1.2.2 Equity

The concept of equity developed to address gaps and deficiencies in the common law, and is rooted in an underlying concept of 'fairness'. For example, the common law did not recognise certain concepts, such as uses and trusts, and its remedies were limited in scope and flexibility, as it relied mainly on the remedy of damages in the form of monetary compensation. Sometimes monetary compensation was an inadequate remedy, as it could not, for example, restore parties making some kind of 'deal', where the 'deal' did not work out as planned, to the position they were in before they attempted to make a deal. Equity was developed to provide non-monetary remedies to moderate the harshness of the common law, such as injunctions (forbidding a specific act), orders of specific performance (imposing an obligation to act), and restitution (where parties are returned to the position from which they started). These are still used today in the area of contract law. Equity cases were dealt with on a flexible basis with an overriding concern for a fair result, rather than the application of rigid principles of law. Equitable remedies are discretionary, and where equity and the common law came into conflict, equity prevailed. This was established formally in the *Judicature Acts* of 1873 and 1875. Equity developed alongside common law and was responsible for the development of law relating to trusts.

1.2.3 English legislation

Acts of Parliament

Formal laws (also referred to as legislation or statutes) can be enacted (i.e., made enforceable) only by a body which has the constitutional right and power to do so. In the United Kingdom, this is the UK Parliament. In this context, United Kingdom refers to England, Wales and Northern Ireland. Scotland has is own legal system. UK legislation is in the form of Acts of Parliament. The normal procedure for implementing legislation involves first a green paper, which is an outline proposal, and then a white paper, which is a more detailed indication of the proposed legislation. Both green and white papers are also referred to as command papers. The House of Commons will then consider a Bill, which is essentially a draft Act. The procedure involves a first reading, where the title is read out; a second reading where a vote is taken; the committee stage, where the Bill is considered in detail; the report stage, when the committee reports back to the House; and a third reading, when a final vote is taken. If approved, the Bill will go forward to the House of Lords where a similar procedure is followed. The House of Lords may delay passage of a Bill into an Act, but cannot prevent it. When the Act receives the formal Royal Assent from the reigning monarch, it becomes law.

There are some exceptions to this procedure, for example, in relation to the Finance Act, which follows a budget speech. Also, some Acts do not come into effect immediately they receive Royal Assent as they allow time for people and bodies who will be affected by them to make changes to their circumstances or otherwise adjust. For example, the *Companies Act 2006* was implemented in stages, with some of the sections not coming into force until 2009.

An Act remains law unless or until it is repealed or amended by a further Act. Sometimes Acts are not always clear as to their wording, and courts must interpret them as best they can, although they cannot challenge them unless a provision in a UK Act contravenes EU law (see Section 1.2.4), by which the UK agreed to be bound when it joined the European Union (as it now is) in 1972. In such a case the UK courts can suspend operation of the UK provision. The courts are permitted to consider the purpose for which any Act was passed and can look at records of Parliamentary debates (Hansard) which occurred before an Act was passed to help determine the meaning of words in the Act.

Delegated legislation

Parliament may delegate some of its legislative powers to other bodies, by passing an enabling Act. Such an Act sets out Parliament's policy and objectives, but then allows another body to develop the detailed rules, which are referred to as delegated legislation. Examples of delegated legislation are statutory instruments (SIs) produced by government ministers in particular departments (e.g., the Treasury); bye-laws produced by local authorities and certain public bodies (e.g., transport authorities such as the London Underground); certain laws which regional parliaments are allowed to make in respect of their own regions; and emergency legislation produced by the Crown and Privy Council.

The courts (as well as certain specific supervisory bodies) have supervisory powers over delegated legislation and can hold that delegated legislation is *ultra vires* (beyond powers conferred in an enabling Act) and so void (of no legal effect). However, the body of delegated legislation introduced each year is immense, so detailed scrutiny of it all is impossible.

Activity 1.2 ....

Visit the website of the UK Parliament, via the link on the B291 website. Browse the site to find out what, for example, the House of Commons does, especially in terms of legislation.

1.2.4   European law

In 1972 the UK joined the European Community (EC) (now called the European Union (EU)), which brought with it an obligation to conform to existing and future EU law. For example, the introduction in the UK of Value Added Tax (VAT) was a direct result of the UK joining the EC. Although there is a European Parliament (EP), it does not have the same role in implementing legislation that the UK Parliament has, as it is not a direct law maker, but rather has a supervisory role over EU institutions. The role of law maker is fulfilled by the Council of Ministers (the Council), which is the main legislative and decision making arm of the EU. The EP has a role in the passing of legislation, as under the 'co-decision' procedure the Council is required to consult with the EP and reach agreement over its legislative proposals, with the EP having the final right of veto. The Council consists of a representative minister from each of the Member States, but membership is determined by any given issue. For example, finance ministers will attend on finance issues, and so forth. The Council acts on the basis of proposals put forward by the European Commission (also simply referred to as the Commission), which is the executive arm of the EU. It also implements legislation and decisions.

There are several sources of EU law, as discussed below.

- **Treaties** are the primary source of law, such as the Treaty of Rome which created the first EC bodies. They automatically become law in member states.

- **Regulations** of the Council and Commission are also directly applicable to member states.

- **Directives** from the Commission and Council are addressed to one or more member states and require them to achieve specified results within an identified time period, which may mean that they must change their own laws so as to comply. In the UK, this may be done by allowing government ministers to implement delegated legislation or by an Act of Parliament.

- **Decisions** can be addressed by the Commission on various issues to individuals or companies, which are binding, but only on those to whom/which they are addressed.

- **Recommendations** and **opinions** may be issued by the Council and the Commission. While they have no legal force, they are persuasive in effect.

- **The European Court of Justice** is the judicial arm of the EU. It comprises judges from the Member States and is the final court for judging all questions and disputes involving EU law. Its decisions are binding on parties who come before it.

Activity 1.3   ....

Visit the website of the European Council, via the link on the B291 website. Browse the site to explore the functions of the Council.

1.2.5   Other sources of law

Lawyers will only resort to other sources of law if none of the previously outlined sources exists. If there is no precedent in English law which applies to a case being heard in an English court, barristers may seek to apply a precedent decided by a court in another common law jurisdiction, especially a Commonwealth country. If this can be regarded as an accurate application of English law, then the court is likely to allow it. The court will sometimes, too, accept the opinion of a textbook writer as to how the law should be applied if there is no other source, but this is very rare.

Legal practitioners

In most countries persons accused of a crime or sued in a civil action, as well as those bringing a case as prosecutor or claimant, have the right to be represented by a qualified legal practitioner or advocate. England and Wales have two kinds of practitioners – solicitors and barristers – who receive different kinds of training, and can act in different types of legal actions and courts. A barrister must be a member of one of the four Inns of Court and will typically appear in cases heard in the Crown Court, the High Court, the Court of Appeal and the Supreme Court, though in certain instances solicitors may also appear in the Crown Court and the High Court (see Section 1.2.6 on the English courts).

Each country has a different system in respect of legal practitioners. Scotland has a different system of advocacy from England and Wales. In the USA, lawyers are referred to as 'attorneys' or 'attorneys-at-law'. The USA is a federal system, with no nationwide qualification for lawyers. Rather, each state sets its own criteria for permission to sit the state Bar Examination. Additionally, nearly all states require candidates to pass the Multistate Bar Examination (MBE) and the Multistate Professional Responsibility Examination (MPRE). Some states also require the passing of the Multistate Essay Examination (MEE) and/or the Multistate Performance Test (MPT).

1.2.6   The doctrine of judicial precedent and the hierarchy of the courts

Section 1.2.1 referred to the doctrine of judicial precedent as a means to ensure certainty, whereby the principles emerging from cases judged in the higher courts are binding on lower courts. Because this process also helps develop principles to meet changing circumstances, it was stated above that, for this reason, common law is sometimes referred to as 'case law' or 'judge-made law', so the cases themselves form a source of law.

The underlying basis of judicial precedent is that of *stare decisis*, which is Latin, meaning literally 'to stand by things decided', and the whole concept is inextricably tied up with the concept of the hierarchy of courts, that is, the idea that some courts are superior to others. Most countries have a court system which has superior and lower courts. As an example of this, the current UK court hierarchy is shown in Figure 1.

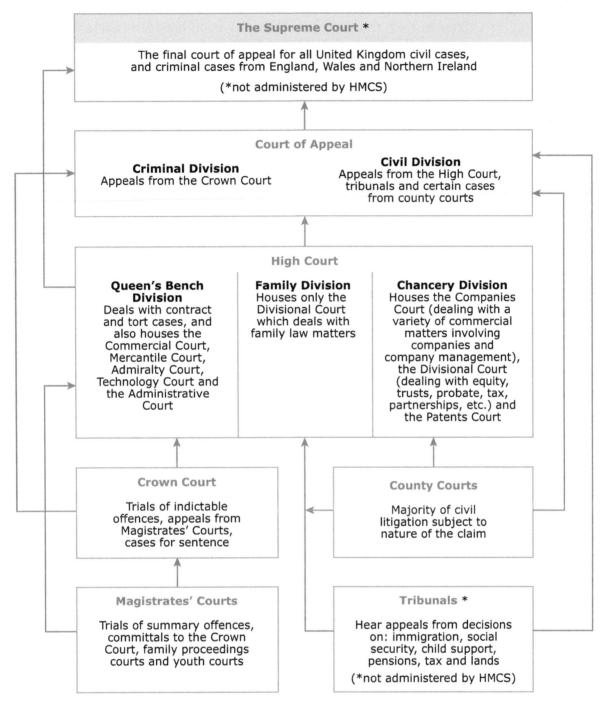

Note: The Supreme Court was formerly the House of Lords in its judicial function. This change occurred as at 1 October 2009.

Figure 1 UK court structure.
Source: Adapted from her Majesty's Courts Service (HMCS) website at www.hmcourts-service.gov.uk/aboutus/structure/index.htm (accessed 9 September 2010).

The arrows in Figure 1 show where a case may be referred to a higher court, either automatically because of the nature of the proceedings or by way of appeal. Appeal procedures can be complex, and only the basic ones are outlined in this section. In certain circumstances, a referral or appeal to a higher court can 'leap frog' over an intermediate stage.

You will see that there is a basic division between courts which deal with civil actions and courts which deal with criminal prosecutions. The majority of civil cases start in the County Court but if a significant amount of money is involved, they may start in the appropriate division of the High Court. Each of the three High Court divisions specialises in particular areas of law, but they also have within them other specialist functions. Appeals may be made from the County and High Court to the Court of Appeal (Civil Division) and from the Court of Appeal and the High Court to the Supreme Court (formerly the House of Lords), but only where the appeal involves a point of law of general public significance. If disputes involve matters of European law, then any courts below the Supreme Court may, and the Supreme Court must, refer the issue to the European Court of Justice for a preliminary ruling as to how European law should be interpreted and applied in this instance.

You will see that tribunals form part of the court structure. They hear appeals from decisions made by government departments, for example, on immigration, or can be dedicated to particular issues, such as employment (see Section 4.3.2), and the right of appeal from a tribunal decision is similar to that of an appeal from the County Court.

All criminal cases start in the Magistrates' Courts, which has two roles. It may try less serious cases by itself (this is known as a summary trial, as the magistrates themselves form a judgment without a jury). Most criminal cases are dealt with in this way. However, if the case is more serious, the Magistrates' Court will decide whether the accused has a case to answer and, if so, will send the case to be tried (a process called a committal) in the Crown Court by a judge and jury. This is what is meant by an offence being indictable, namely, it goes to be tried by a judge and jury. (Note that not all countries have a jury system. Even some of those that do have a jury system will not use a jury for all types of trials.) From the Magistrates' Court and Crown Court, appeal by way of case stated is to the Divisional Court of the Queen's Bench Division. 'Case stated' means that the findings of fact and law made by the Magistrates' and Crown Court are stated in writing and sent to the higher court which decides whether or not the law has been correctly applied. If not, the case will be referred back to the Magistrates' or Crown Court, which will be required to apply the law as determined by the higher court. The Court of Appeal (Criminal Division) hears other appeals from the Crown Court and the Supreme Court hears appeals from the Court of Appeal or the Divisional Court involving points of law that are generally of public importance.

Different types of judges operate in different courts (e.g., circuit judges and district judges in the County Court; High Court or puisne (pronounce 'puny') judges in the High Court; the Master of the Rolls and the Lord Chief Justices of Appeal in the Court of Appeal; the Lords of Appeal in Ordinary (Law Lords) in the Supreme Court, etc.). The Privy Council (usually, but not always, in the form of five Lords of Appeal in Ordinary) acts as a final court of appeal for Commonwealth countries which still have this court as the court of final appeal.

It is common for 'judgment' in relation to legal cases to be spelt without the middle 'e' (found in another, accepted spelling, namely, 'judgement'), and this practice is adopted in Unit 7.

It would appear that the term 'Law Lord' is still used to describe judges in the Supreme Court, despite the official term now being 'Justice of the Supreme Court'.

In a court case, a judge does the following:

- examines the facts and identifies those which are material (essential to his/her decision);
- considers the law relating to the material facts; and
- applies the law to the facts and gives a decision.

You have already done this yourself in Activity 1.1 in considering what happened with Derek, Gnasher and Humphrey. However, significant parts of the formal judgment process are the *ratio decidendi* and the *obiter dicta*.

Ratio decidendi is Latin for 'reason of (= for) deciding', and is the underlying legal principle or reason for the judge coming to the decision he/she did, based on the material facts and how the law applies to those facts. *Obiter dicta* are Latin words meaning 'things said otherwise' and refer to general comments the judge makes. It can sometimes be difficult in formal case reports to distinguish the *ratio decidendi* from the *obiter dicta*.

Decisions in previous cases may provide precedents of different levels of importance. A binding precedent must legally be followed by a court deciding on a later case, whereas a court is not legally bound to follow a persuasive precedent, though it will usually do so. This all ties in to the court hierarchy in that the decisions of a lower court will follow the previous decisions of a higher court, in general, as shown in Table 2 below.

Table 2 Order of case precedence

Supreme Court (formerly the House of Lords)	Decisions bind all lower courts where cases have the same material facts. It can deviate from its own earlier decisions, as you will learn a little later.
The Court of Appeal	Bound by Supreme Court decisions, and by its own earlier decisions, unless a decision was reached without due care (termed *per incuriam*) or there are contradictory previous decisions.
High Court	Bound by Supreme Court decisions and Court of Appeal decisions, but not by its own previous decisions.
County Court	Bound by decisions of all higher courts, at the highest level at which a case was decided, but not by previous County Court decisions.

As well as becoming a precedent, a case may also cease to be a precedent. This may occur in the same case if one of the parties in a case appeals to a higher court, following a decision in a lower court. The higher court can then overturn the decision of the lower court case between those parties, and the higher court decision will then stand as a precedent. A higher court can also overrule the earlier decision of a lower court when a different case is decided (i.e., different in that the parties are not the same as those involved in that earlier case), although that earlier, lower court decision will still be valid for the parties involved. A later court can also decide that the facts of a case are different from any earlier case, so the earlier case decision will not be used as a precedent. If this is done, the newer case is said to be distinguished on the facts. It would be fair to say that judges have sometimes been creative in distinguishing the facts of newer cases when they thought that applying a precedent case would give an undesirable effect, and this is regarded as one of the disadvantages of the common law system.

In common law, where not all law is codified, deciding cases by reference to past, similar ones, however, is logical and necessary to make the system workable at all. The purpose of precedent is to strike a balance between flexibility and rigidity. The law needs principles which are certain and applicable to specific situations, but which are adaptable and capable of development to meet the changing needs of society. For something to be both flexible and rigid is conceptually difficult, as these ideas conflict. Certainty is at odds with the notion of allowing law to change and grow. Also it places a limit on judicial discretion. Such problems had been recognised and debated since the mid-1800s, but it was not until 1966 that the House of Lords (now the Supreme Court) was formally allowed to overrule its earlier decisions. It notified this change of stance in a *Practice Statement* on judicial precedent ([1966] 1 WLR 1234). This stated that while the Lords would treat their own former decisions as 'normally binding, they would depart from a decision when it appear[ed] right to do so' ([1966] 1 WLR 1234, paragraph 2). Importantly, it limited such a right of departure to itself: it was not intended to apply to other, lower courts. Academic writers have commented variously on the legal validity of this statement.

Activity 1.4

Visit the home page of the UK Supreme Court, via the link on the B291 website.
Read about the history of the Supreme Court.

In consequence of the 1966 *Practice Statement*, Lord Denning, a famous English judge, for many years campaigned for it to apply also in the Court of Appeal. The climax of this campaign was the case of *Davis v Johnson* [1979] AC 264. Lord Denning was prepared to say that, as earlier cases did not provide a right principle (or *ratio decidendi*) by which to judge this case, he was prepared to lay down the right principle. However, only two of his four fellow judges in the case agreed, though for a different reason (that adhering to precedent would create injustice in this particular case). On appeal to the Lords this majority verdict was rejected, and the Court of Appeal was sternly advised to adhere to its own previous decisions.

Legal terminology and case references

In the titles or names of cases, the name of the party prosecuting or bringing the action (claimant, formerly plaintiff) appears first. The second name is that of the accused or the defendant. The use of 'v' between the two names denotes the adversarial nature of the legal process. Please note that this is usually pronounced 'and' and NEVER 'vee' or 'versus'. The latter pronunciations are confined to sporting fixtures. You will also see a set of numbers and/or letters following a case name, as in the reference to *Davis v Johnson* above, namely '[1979] AC 264'. This is the reference to the set of law reports in which the case was formally reported. Sometimes cases are reported in several different sets of reports, and the different sets of reports have conventions for referencing. There is a usually a date (which may be in round or square brackets), although some older case reports do not have a date. Often there is a volume number, together with an abbreviation of the name of the reports (e.g., 'AC' stands for 'Appeal Cases') which sometimes gives an indication of the court, or level of court, in which the case reported was heard, and a page number, which indicates where in a particular set of reports or volumes the case report begins. Conventions on reporting cases differ between countries.

When referring to cases and Acts of Parliament (or other legislation), for eTMAs you should use exactly the same way of referencing that is used in this unit. This is because doing an eTMA allows you sufficient time to look things up and make sure that you get them right. However, in the unseen examination, it would be sufficient to give just the name and date of a case or legislation, and there will be no need in such circumstances to be concerned with square or round brackets or italics.

1.3 Different legal systems

We have seen so far that the English legal system is a mixture of common law, evolved from customary law, and specific, written (codified) law. It has developed over a long period of time, and has been subject to many influences, such as Roman law and mediaeval Norman-French law, as a result of historical events, such as the Roman and Norman invasions. The legal systems of most countries will display a similarly complex history with elements of several traditions/systems, but many countries reveal an adherence more to one legal tradition than another, which is often deliberate. There are generally four legal traditions that can be observed worldwide, and these are discussed below, along with international law (see Figure 2). Some systems are more difficult to classify than others, for example, that of China, which is in a state of on-going development.

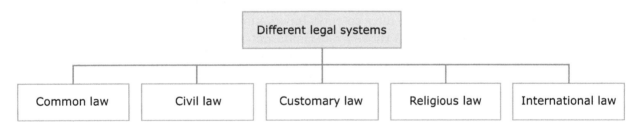

Figure 2   Different legal systems

1.3.1   Common law

This is often referred to as an Anglo-Saxon legal tradition, and we have discussed this in relation to the UK, in terms of the way that law is developed through cases which create precedents. Australia, Canada (excluding Quebec) and the United States are also regarded as common law systems, though the US state of Louisiana uses both common law and Napoleonic civil law (see Section 1.3.2), which reflects its French origin. This categorisation does not mean, however, that these countries do not have written laws as well. Common law systems also help, arguably, to develop written law as case decisions can help determine how written law is to be interpreted and/or applied.

1.3.2 Civil law

In this context, civil law should not be confused with the civil law (distinct from criminal law) that defines rights and duties between citizens. When civil law refers to a legal tradition or system, it means that the law is codified, that is, there is a comprehensive system of written rules that are interpreted and applied by judges. (It is therefore sometimes also referred to as a civil code or code law, and, confusingly, will include criminal law as well.) Only these written rules are considered binding, but not precedent cases as in common law. This is the most important difference between civil law and common law systems. However, for consistency and practicality, the decisions in previous cases will be followed.

Civil law systems are the most common systems of law worldwide. They originate in Roman law, which was adopted by many countries in the late Middle Ages. However, many modern systems were influenced by the nineteenth century move towards codified systems as exemplified in the French *Code de Napoléon*, which had a particular impact on Latin American countries and former French and Spanish colonies. Often a national codified system contains different codes for different areas of law, such as in respect of tax or businesses. These are often named by reference to the type of law they deal with, for example, criminal code, civil code, securities and exchange code, commercial code and tax code. Currently, France has a codified system (the *Code Civil*, dating from 1904) for all aspects of its law, except tort (see Session 2). Most European countries now have wholly or predominantly codified law, except Denmark, which has a system not unlike the English one.

1.3.3 Customary law

Essentially a customary law system is one which evolves in a particular country to address the needs of a particular culture or cultures. It may co-exist harmoniously with other legal systems, especially if those systems do not regulate the areas governed by customary law. India, for example, operates mainly a common law system, but includes a significant amount of both customary and religious law. Although English law had its roots in customary law under the Normans, as has been mentioned, it grew into something different through its use of judicial precedent in the development of case law.

1.3.4 Religious law

Some countries base their law on a system of religious beliefs. The most widespread form of such law is Sharia law (Islamic/Muslim law), although there are still regions which practise Christian canon (or church) law, whether Anglican, Catholic or Eastern Orthodox. Similarly, Orthodox and Conservative Jews practise *halakha* (or *halacha*) in different forms.

Most religious law is concerned with church or religious matters, but Sharia law is more extensive. There are two primary sources of Sharia law – the Qur'an (the holy text of the Muslim faith), and the Sunnah (the Way, the sayings and example set by the Prophet Mohammad). *Fiqh*, or jurisprudence, interprets and extends Sharia law to matters not directly addressed by the primary sources, by including secondary sources which are usually agreed opinions of religious scholars.

In Muslim societies, the extent to which Sharia law is practised varies, as does its interpretation and implementation. Some countries, where a large part of the population practises the Muslim faith, only apply Sharia law in the area of family law, but otherwise have non-religious/secular laws, for example, Pakistan, Bangladesh and Indonesia. Other countries have a greater mixture of religious and secular laws, such as those in North Africa and the Middle East. Turkey, however, has a large Muslim population, but a wholly secular legal system. Cyprus has a very mixed system which includes, among other elements, specific legislation, common law, Muslim law, Ecclesiastical Greek Orthodox law and EU law. Malaysia, while predominantly a common law system, has Islamic law which applies to Muslims.

In addition to family law, Sharia law extends to financial and commercial transactions, peace, warfare and penal punishments. The overall intention of Sharia law is that people should live in harmony in a just society, but the extent and intensity to which Sharia regulations are applied to achieve this does generate considerable differences, and indeed, controversy, especially in the areas of punishment for breaking the law, freedom of speech, conversion to another religion, dietary laws and the role of women.

1.3.5　International law

We have seen that individual countries have their own internal laws. However, countries do not exist in isolation, and there is a significant body of international law, which regulates the dealings between sovereign states and their rights and duties in regard to each other. This is referred to as **public international law** and deals with such matters as the formation and recognition of states, acquisition of territory, wars, the law of the sea and of space, treatment of aliens, human rights, international crimes and international settlement of disputes. Certain international organisations, such as the United Nations, may have rights and duties under international law. **Private international law** establishes rules for dealing with cases where a foreign element is involved, where there is contact with the law of another country, for example, if a contract (see Session 3) is made in England but is to be fulfilled abroad.

The primary sources of international law are generally accepted to be: international custom (in so far as this is evidence of a general practice of behaviour that is accepted as legally binding); **treaties** or **conventions**; and general principles of law as recognised by civilised nations. However, as these general principles are often those which appear to underlie European and US laws, their relevance and application to developing or socialist countries is sometimes thought to be contentious. Sometimes an agreement between one or more states will necessitate the enactment of domestic legislation to implement the agreement. We have considered some of this in relation to the EU, but another good example is the *European Convention on Human Rights*, which has been given effect in the UK by the *Human Rights Act 1998*, and which has had a significant effect on many existing aspects of UK law.

Summary

In this session you have learned about the difference between civil and criminal law, and the sources of English law (as a common law system), including case law and the doctrine of judicial precedent. You have seen how legal systems differ by considering also codified (civil law) systems, customary law, religious law and international legal regulations. This session provided a background for the further study of different elements of law that relate more specifically to business situations and/or business dealings between individuals or entities. In Session 2, we will start by looking at the law of tort in this context.

SESSION **2 The law of tort**

Introduction

Upon completion of Session 2 you are expected to be able to:

- understand the concept of tort, especially the tort of negligence
- understand the essential elements of duty of care, breach of that duty, damage, loss, injury and liability
- explain and discuss negligence in relation to professional advisers.

In Session 2 you will learn how tort is one of the areas of civil law that is relevant to business.

2.1 Defining tort and its principal elements

A tort is a civil wrong (distinct from a crime, a breach of contract and a breach of trust). The concept of tort is not confined to English or UK law, but is recognised by all main legal systems, though they may deal with it differently. There are many aspects of tort, such as various forms of trespass, defamation (slander and libel), nuisance, liability for animals, etc., but the aspect of tort that most concerns business is that of negligence, and we shall concentrate on this. Negligence often has financial implications for businesses, for example, in the outcome (actual and potential) of a court case, and accountants need to be able to deal with them. Also, in their role as advisers, accountants may themselves be charged with negligence (see Section 2.5). In England, negligence is a common law offence, but some aspects of it are dealt with now in specific statutes, such as the *Occupiers' Liability Act 1957*, the *Sale of Goods Act 1979* and the *Consumer Protection Act 1987*. Negligence can only exist if the claimant is owed a duty of care, if the defendant is guilty of a breach of that duty and if damage has been caused to the claimant by that breach. The claimant must prove that he/she has suffered damage. We shall look at these various elements in turn.

2.2 Duty of care

If it is reasonably foreseeable that your actions are likely to affect someone, then it is likely that you owe that person a duty of care. This is the so-called 'neighbour test' that was set out in the well known case of *Donoghue v Stevenson* [1932] AC 562. In this case, Mrs Donoghue's friend purchased in a café a bottle of ginger beer, which the friend gave to Mrs Donoghue. The ginger beer was in an opaque bottle, which had been sealed by the manufacturer. Mrs Donoghue drank some of the contents, but when the friend poured the remainder into Mrs Donoghue's glass, it contained the remnants of a decomposed snail. As a result, Mrs Donoghue became seriously ill. Mrs Donoghue did not herself buy the bottle so had no claim against the café, so she could not sue the café for a breach of contract (which would normally have been the usual way to obtain a legal remedy where someone had purchased something which caused harm), so she sued the manufacturer of the ginger beer for negligence. This is a key case, as it was the first time that such a claim in tort had succeeded. The House of Lords held that a manufacturer of goods had a duty of care not only to the buyer of those goods, but also to anyone else who might reasonably be foreseen to suffer physical injury resulting from defects which they contained. Lord Atkin, one of the five judges in the case said:

> You must take reasonable care to avoid acts or omissions which you can reasonably see would be likely to injure your neighbour. Who then in law is my neighbour? The answer seems to be persons who are so closely and directly affected by my act that I ought reasonably to have them in contemplation as being so affected when I am directing my mind to the acts or omission which are called into question.
>
> [1932] AC 562, at 580

Another judge, Lord Macmillan, added:

> The law takes no cognizance of carelessness in the abstract. It concerns itself with carelessness only where there is a duty to take care and where failure in that duty has caused damage.
>
> [1932] AC 562, at 618

Many later cases have extended the duty of care beyond one's 'neighbours' in the sense meant by Lord Atkin. In *Anns v Merton London Borough Council* [1978] AC 728, a two step guideline was set out to determine whether or not a duty of care existed in particular circumstances. The claimants were lessees of flats which they claimed had suffered structural deterioration because the foundations were of insufficient depth. They sued the local authority for negligence on the basis that it had failed to inspect the foundations, or had been negligent when it had done so. Lord Wilberforce raised two issues:

1 As between the alleged wrongdoer and the injured party there must be a relationship of proximity or neighbourhood, such that in reasonable contemplation of the former, carelessness on his part may be likely to cause damage to the latter, in which case a prima facie duty of care arises.

2 If the question is answered affirmatively, it is necessary to consider whether there are any considerations which ought to negative [*sic*], or reduce or limit the scope of the duty or class of persons to whom it is owed.

[1978] AC 728, at 751

This extended the number of third parties to whom a duty of care is owed, in circumstances involving non-physical injury. The *Anns* judgment was regarded as controversial and as an attempt to develop a general duty of care, and was overruled in the case of *Murphy v Brentwood District Council* [1990] 1 AC 398, a case with very similar facts to *Anns* although it was applied in a case involving financial loss and professional negligence (see Section 2.5).

In *Caparo Industries plc v Dickman and Others* [1990] 2 AC 605, the House of Lords considered that a three part test needed to be satisfied to establish that a duty of care exists, with the following elements.

1   Foreseeability of damage.

2   Proximity of relationship.

3   Fairness. The court must consider it fair, just and reasonable to impose a duty of care.

This meant that, in future cases, all three of the above requirements would need to be satisfied to establish a duty of care, regardless of the nature of the damage. This was determined in the case of *Marc Rich & Co v Bishop Rock Marine Co Ltd* [1996] AC 211 which involved a ship sinking after being declared fit to complete a voyage if necessary welding were done (which it was).

Arguments have frequently been put forward that a boundary must be drawn around the law of negligence otherwise there would be: (a) a flood of claims (the so-called 'floodgates' argument); and (b) continuing uncertainty about the legal consequences of going about our daily lives. This argument has been applied with considerable force to the areas of economic loss and psychiatric harm (see Section 2.4).

Public policy too may be significant in this area. The courts may rule that public authorities should be immune from claims for negligence. The arguments for immunity are that: (a) imposition of a duty of care would inevitably result in breaches and consequent legal actions, which would divert resources from the provision of the service and into litigation; (b) the risk of litigation would encourage an over-cautious and defensive attitude towards service provision; and (c) the outcome might be absurd and/or undesirable. On the other hand, injured parties would be deprived of their human rights by not having a legal remedy. The National Health Service in the UK is not immune but there are those who think it should be. Recent case law has tended to be in favour of restricting public immunity. For example, the police's blanket immunity in *Osman v UK* [1999] 1 FLR 193 was found to be a breach of the *European Convention for Human Rights* (Article 6, the right to a fair trial).

Activity 2.1

A player at a cricket match hit a cricket ball over a 17 foot high fence. The ball hit Mrs Patel, who was standing on the pavement outside her house. The ball travelled about 100 yards. Such a thing had happened only about six times in 30 years.

Does the cricket club owe a duty of care to Mrs Patel?

Feedback

No duty of care is owed. The risk of something like this happening was so slight and the expense of reducing it so great that a reasonable cricket club would not have taken any further precautions. (These are essentially the facts and decision in *Bolton v Stone* [1851] AC 580.)

2.3 Breach of duty

A defendant will discharge (i.e., carry out) his/her duty of care if the degree of care exercised is that which a reasonable person would have exercised. This will, of course, vary with the circumstances of any case. Relevant factors which have been taken into account in cases include the magnitude of a foreseeable risk of harm being caused; the known characteristics of the party exposed to the risk of harm (e.g., some disability); whether the defendant was faced with an emergency; whether there was a particular relationship between parties, such as that of competitor to spectator; and the state of health of the defendant. Employers, who have statutory and contractual duties towards their employees, also have a common law duty to act with reasonable care, for example, in the provision of competent staff to do a job, provision of proper tools, machinery and premises and provision of a safe system of work and supervision. Under the concept of vicarious liability, an employer will be liable for the torts of an employee that are committed within the course of the employment, that is, where the tortious act committed is a wrongful way of doing what the employee is employed to do. In *Limpus v London General Omnibus Co* (1862) 1 H&C 526, a bus driver disobeyed an instruction not to race with or obstruct the buses of rival companies. He caused an accident in which the claimant's horses were injured. His employers were held liable as this was regarded as an improper way adopted by the employee to do his job. In general, those who are in positions of responsibility are expected to exercise a greater duty of care. Greater care, in general, must be exercised towards more vulnerable individuals, such as children. Children, however, are allowed to show a lower duty of care. The more serious the consequences of a lack of care are, the greater the care that should be taken.

Usually the claimant will need to prove a breach of duty, but in certain circumstances this will not be so, namely, that of *res ipsa loquitur*, which is Latin for 'the thing speaks for itself'. In such a case, the normal burden of proof is reversed and the defendant is required to prove that he/she has not been negligent. This may occur when the 'thing' in question is under the defendant's control, when the defendant has knowledge denied to the claimant, or the damage is such that it would not normally have happened if the defendant had exercised proper care. In the case of *Mahon v Osborne* [1939] 2 KB 14, for example, a patient discovered after an abdominal operation that surgical swabs had been left inside him, hence the surgeon was required to prove that he had not been negligent.

Activity 2.2

Henry is a tyre fitter and damaged his back heaving very heavy tyres on to his employer's truck. The mechanical hoist was broken so Henry had lifted the tyres manually, and when loading the seventh tyre he suffered a slipped disc in his back. His employer argued that the manoeuvre did not require use of a hoist. Allegedly, the hoist had been out of order for two years.

Was a duty of care owed to Henry?

If so, was there a breach of the duty?

Was it reasonably foreseeable that a breach would cause injury?

Did any breach actually cause injury?

Would it have made any difference if the hoist had been out of order for only two days?

Would it have made any difference if his employer had instructed Henry not to lift tyres on his own?

Feedback ....

Was a duty of care owed to Henry? Yes – an employer owes a duty of care to an employee.

If so, was there a breach of the duty? Yes – there was an unsafe system of working, and an employer has a duty to provide a safe system.

Was it reasonably foreseeable that a breach would cause injury? Yes.

Did any breach actually cause injury? Yes.

Would it have made any difference if the hoist had been out of order for only two days? Probably not – the answers above are still the same.

Would it have made any difference if his employer had instructed Henry not to lift tyres on his own? Yes – Henry would have been partly to blame through his own negligence (= **contributory negligence,** which is discussed in Section 2.3.1).[2]

A court would be likely to award Henry damages for loss of earnings and for pain and suffering caused.

2.3.1   Defences to a charge of negligence

There are several possible lines of defence to a charge of negligence, as follows.

- *Volenti non fit injuria*. This is Latin and means 'injury cannot be done to one who is willing', that is, to one who consents expressly or implicitly to suffer actual harm or to run the risk of it. Consent given under protest or duress is not valid consent. Apparent consent can be negated by statute. For example, a passenger does not agree to travel at his/her own risk simply because the *Road Traffic Act 1982* makes passenger insurance compulsory.

- Causation. This is concerned with the factors leading to an event. If the claimant would have suffered the same injury despite the defendant's conduct, then the defendant will not be liable. The concept of contributory negligence is also relevant here. If the claimant is partly responsible for his/her own misfortune, then the courts have discretion to reduce the amount of damages awarded accordingly. In the case of *Froom v Butcher* [1976] 2 QB 286, the claimant sustained head and chest injuries in a traffic collision caused by the defendant, which would have been prevented if the claimant had been wearing a seat belt. Because the claimant failed to take reasonable precautions for his own safety, his damages were reduced accordingly. However, if causation is established and the basic elements of tort are proved, the defendant may be able to prove that there was not a sufficiently close connection between his/her behaviour and the damage the claimant suffered (in line with the idea of 'reasonable

---

[2] You might be wondering what the difference is between the decision in *Limpus v London General Omnibus Co*, discussed earlier, and Henry's situation, as the issue of contributory negligence was not raised in *Limpus*. While a company employee in that case disobeyed an employer's instruction, a third party suffered damage, not the employee. Contributory negligence only applies where someone does something he/she should not and injures himself/herself, rather than a third party. As an employer is vicariously liable for the acts of employees, if the latter disobey instructions, they may themselves expect to be disciplined, possibly fired or even face criminal charges, depending on the nature of their action.

foreseeability', as discussed earlier in this session). For this reason, causation is linked to the idea of remoteness.

Sometimes a loss may result as a consequence of a chain of events occurring, with a 'new event intervening' (*novus actus interveniens*) between an original event and the ultimate damage. Again the test applied here will be that of forseeability/remoteness.

The claimant must be taken as the defendant finds him/her, even if the condition of the claimant means the loss or damage suffered was not reasonably foreseeable. A claimant's medical condition unknown at the time of harm/damage, for example, cannot be used as a defence. In *Smith v Leech Brain & Co* [1962] 2 QB 405, the claimant employee suffered a burn to his lip as a result of inadequate safety procedures in the defendant employer's factory. His lip was in a pre-cancerous condition and the burn caused him to develop cancer which ultimately led to his death. The defendant was held liable, as the key question was whether the burn could have been foreseen (which it could), not whether the cancer could have been foreseen. This is sometimes referred to as the 'eggshell skull' principle, that is, a defendant cannot use a victim's existing physical condition to his/her own advantage as a defence to the charge brought.

- There are sometimes other general defences which may apply. In rare circumstances, where mistakes are made that result in false imprisonment, unwarranted (also termed 'malicious') prosecution or unintentional defamation, the defence of (having made a genuine) mistake can apply. There are also circumstances in which claiming that harm occurred as a result of an inevitable accident, an Act of God, self-defence or necessity (i.e., attempting to prevent greater damage to self than was inflicted on an innocent claimant) may be available to a defendant.

You should also be aware of the concept of strict liability. This is where liability is imposed without the claimant having to prove that the defendant was at fault. It is exceptional in tort, but would be imposed, for example, for damage done by trespassing livestock, or dogs not kept under proper control. (It would actually be imposed in those cases by statute, respectively the *Animals Act 1971* and the *Dangerous Dogs Act 1991*. You have already encountered the latter in Activity 1.1.)

Activity 2.3 ....

Mr Webb, disregarding his employer's safety instructions, was riding on the tow-bar of one of his employer's commercial vehicles, when another employee negligently drove into the back of the vehicle and injured him. Mr Webb feels he will have an action for negligence and an expectation of damages, as the obvious risk associated with riding on the tow-bar was of being thrown off, not being crushed by another vehicle running into him from behind. Advise Mr Webb of his chances of success. Would your advice differ, if, say, instead of being hit by another vehicle, Mr Webb had been struck in the eye by a shot fired by a negligent sportsman?

Feedback ....

> Despite the negligence of the other driver, Mr Webb's behaviour would appear to have been partly responsible for his misfortune. As well as being thrown off, it is also possible in the circumstances that another vehicle would run into him from behind. There is a sufficiently close connection between his behaviour and the damage he suffered. While Mr Webb's claim would be likely to succeed, the court would be equally likely to reduce any damages awarded because of his contributory negligence.
>
> However, if he had been hit in the eye by a shot fired by a negligent sportsman, the connection between this and his own behaviour would be remote. His carelessness would be likely to be deemed irrelevant and not affect any award of damages. (This was the opinion, at least, of Lord Denning, in the case of *Jones v Livox Quarries Ltd* [1952] 2 QB 608, on which the facts of this activity are based.)

2.4 Damage caused

So far we have not considered specifically the types of harm that can be caused in tort, especially in relation to negligence. These are:

- physical harm
- nervous shock/psychiatric harm
- damage to property
- economic loss.

It was clear in the *Donoghue v Stevenson* (see Section 2.2) case that physical harm had been caused to Mrs Donoghue. Physical harm to a person may also result in harm to his/her property, for example, a vehicle damaged in a traffic accident. Nervous shock/psychiatric harm may also be caused in various ways, but this may raise more difficult questions about how it was caused and what was or was not a reasonable standard of care. A principal context for this is employment where an employee may suffer psychiatric harm because of overwork. The leading employment case is *Barber v Somerset County Council* [2004] IRLR 475. However, psychiatric harm may also be caused to a secondary victim, often someone who has witnessed an accident or disaster in which primary victims have suffered death or physical injury. The courts have established rules about when a duty of care applies in *Alcock v Chief Constable of South Yorkshire* [1991] 1 AC 310 (the 'Hillsborough Disaster'). Proximity is required in terms of relationship, time and place.

The usual remedy for harm is damages in the form of money, and this has always included damages for any financial loss directly associated with personal injury or with property (e.g., loss of earnings, repair costs). However, the issue of pure economic/financial loss where there is no physical injury to person or property has proved a vexed issue for the courts and will be considered separately in Section 2.5, as it brings us to the consideration in this respect of accountants, auditors and other professional advisers.

Activity 2.4

Peter is a security officer, employed by a company. While at work on a routine patrol, he witnesses an accident on the company's production line, in which an employee is killed. Peter suffers psychiatric trauma as a consequence.

Does Peter have any basis for a legal action? Would it make any difference if Peter was the father of the employee who was killed or if Peter had witnessed the accident on the security video rather than as it happened?

Feedback

Peter is a secondary victim so the rules in *Alcock v Chief Constable of South Yorkshire* apply. The relationship does not appear close enough for a claim of psychiatric harm to succeed, although it would be if Peter were the father of the employee killed in the accident, or could bring evidence to show a similar relationship based on love/affection. The same criteria would apply if Peter had seen the accident on a security video.

If Peter was a person who was not as mentally tough as most, then there might be a case for arguing the 'eggshell skull' principle, but this is unlikely to succeed, other than in the case of a primary victim. However, one would expect a security guard, perhaps, to be both physically and mentally tough.

2.5 Financial loss, negligence and professional advisers

Financial loss often results from negligent advice, given by professional advisers, such as accountants and auditors, and for a long time the courts were reluctant to extend the 'neighbour' principle to this area, following the 'floodgates' argument expressed in the 1931 US case of *Ultramares Corporation v Touche* 255 NY 170, 174 NE 441 at 179 by Cardozo, CJ, that the law should not admit 'to a liability in an indeterminate amount for an indeterminate time to an indeterminate class'. This view prevailed until 1963.

'CJ' stands for 'Chief Justice'. You will also see, in reference to English cases, 'LJ', which stands for 'Lord Justice' and 'J', which stand for 'Justice'.

The case of *Hedley Byrne & Co Ltd v Heller & Partners Ltd* [1964] AC 465 extended the duty of care to third parties for financial loss where it could be shown that a 'special relationship' exists, that is, where a provider of financial information knows, or ought to know, that a particular person is going to rely on the information for some specific purpose. Hedley Byrne, a firm of advertising agents, wanted to check the creditworthiness of a customer, Easipower Ltd, which had placed a large order. Hedley Byrne asked their bank, National Provincial Bank Ltd, to obtain a report from Easipower's bank, Heller & Partners Ltd, who replied in a letter using the words 'without responsibility on the part of this bank', saying that Easipower was 'considered good for its ordinary business engagements'. Hedley proceeded with the orders and Easipower later went into liquidation. Hedley Byrne lost £17,000 on contracts and sued Heller & Partners for negligence. They claimed that the latter's letter was provided negligently and was misleading. Heller & Partners argued they owed no duty of care in respect of the statements they made, and that, in any case, liability was excluded. However, they were found to be negligent.

This was a landmark case in that it recognised third party liability in a case involving financial loss. Until then, as we have seen, such liability had been limited to situations involving physical injury, although Lord Denning in the case of *Candler v Crane Christmas & Co* [1951] 2 KB 164 had expressed a dissenting view then that accountants owed this type of care to third parties in similar circumstances to the *Hedley Byrne* case.

Cases involving auditors especially were of great importance generally in developing the concept of financial negligence alongside other negligence issues. For example, the 1978 case of *Anns v Merton London Borough Council*, mentioned in Section 2.2, was regarded from a financial perspective as introducing a 'relationship of proximity or neighbourhood' in place of a 'special relationship', and replacing a test of 'knowledge' that someone would actually rely on advice given (and may suffer loss/damage) with one of 'reasonable foreseeability'. These tests were applied in the New Zealand case of *Scott Group v McFarlane* [1978] 1 NZLR 553, which revolved round a particular group of people who were likely to become investors in the company which was being audited.

By the mid-1980s, through numerous cases, the auditors' duty of care was extended, on a case by case basis, to virtually anyone who auditors could, or should, reasonably foresee might rely on audited financial statements when making investment decisions in respect of an entity on which the auditor was reporting. This made the duty of care very wide indeed, given that audited accounts are filed publicly.

'Living down a criminal record'

The 1990 case of *Caparo Industries plc v Dickman and Others*, which has already been discussed in Section 2.2 in terms of defining a duty of care, was also significant in respect of financial loss and negligence as regards auditors, as the House of Lords' judgment again restricted the parties to whom the auditor would owe a duty of care. The case involved an action by a shareholder against the auditors of a company. As many thousands of shareholders and potential shareholders may rely on an auditor's reports, the House of Lords held that it was not practical for an auditor to owe a duty of care to so many individuals. This was the concern that had been expressed in *Ultramares Corporation v Touche*. The Law Lords were unanimous that, in general, auditors do not owe a duty of care to individual shareholders or potential investors: the duty of care is owed to shareholders as a body. It was thus held that *Scott Group v McFarlane* (and other cases decided on principles developed from the *Anns* case) had been wrongly decided. This case seemed to return the law to a position it had been in 30 years previously at the time of *Hedley Byrne*. Some commentators regretted this, as both professional investors and ordinary individual investors would be denied an avenue for relief when they suffered loss as a result of auditors' negligence.

There have been numerous cases subsequent to *Caparo*, which it is impractical to include in detail. The subject of the legal liability of auditors for negligence is extensively addressed in Chapter 15 of *Principles of External Auditing* (Porter et al., 2008), from which (on pp. 624–5) the following synopsis of key points emerging from post-*Caparo* cases has been adapted.

- In addition to the 'three part *Caparo* test' (see Section 2.2), courts may apply a 'voluntary assumption of responsibility test' (where an auditor appears of his/her own accord to take on the responsibility of a duty of care) to decide whether or not an auditor owed a duty of care to a third party.

- The law in respect of auditor liability to third parties for economic loss is transitional and developmental and will only be developed in small steps.

- Where a third party has received independent advice, it will serve to strengthen the barrier between an auditor and the third party. This barrier needs to be overcome before an auditor will be held to owe a duty of care to a third party.

- If a third party claims to have suffered loss as a result of an auditor's negligence, the court will evaluate the facts to determine whether the auditor's negligence caused loss or merely provided an opportunity for the claimant to sustain loss. Only the former will give rise to damages.

- To succeed in a case alleging financial loss caused by auditor negligence, a third party must commence proceedings within a period in which it is reasonably foreseeable that reliance may be placed on audited financial statements.

- Whether or not an auditor will owe a duty of care to one or more parties in a particular case depends on the particular facts of that case. Notwithstanding *Caparo*, courts have decided that auditors may in principle be held to owe a duty of care to, among others, individual shareholders and directors of the company being audited (the auditee); a 'sister' subsidiary company and/or parent company of the auditee; and auditors of a parent company. It was emphasised in each case that each decision was case-specific.

- It may be possible for an auditor to disclaim responsibility to third parties by advising relevant third parties of that disclaimer.

Porter et al. (2008) comment that a more general theme can be detected in the post-*Caparo* cases they review, which was given explicit reference in the New Zealand case of *South Pacific Manufacturing Co Ltd v New Zealand Security Consultants & Investigations Ltd* [1992] 2 NZLR 282. The theme is that proper standards of care should be imposed on people who undertake tasks which require skill and judgement and on whom others depend. This must be balanced by the requirement to maintain an appropriate balance between the different interests of people (e.g., claimants and defendants) in business or daily life. Judges seek to decide, regardless of which case precedent they follow, on the basis of the facts before them in each case, whether it is just and reasonable to impose a duty of care on one party for the benefit of another.

An auditor's defence to a charge of negligence would be to demonstrate that he/she has not been negligent, by demonstrating a high level of skill, competence and use of high quality audit procedures, and by the audit profession showing that it can effectively police itself. However, often claims for negligence have been settled out of court, as a 'least cost option' in terms of money spent on potential payment of damages, court costs, lost time, lost earnings, etc. This was encouraged by professional indemnity insurers (PII), even if auditors could have won their case. A disadvantage of settling out of court is that it stifles development of legal clarity and causes PII premia to rise. It also attracts adverse reports in the media. There have been many suggestions made whereby audit and other professional service firms might limit their financial liability for claims against them. Two that have been implemented have been to allow professional advisory firms to become limited liability partnerships, a topic which was discussed in Unit 1, and to allow an auditee firm and its auditor to have a liability limitation agreement. The latter is now permitted by *s.534* of *Companies Act 2006* and can limit the auditor's financial liability in respect of any negligence, default (failure to comply) or breach of duty to the extent that it is reasonable (*s.537*). At the time of writing this unit, the effect and effectiveness of these provisions are still unknown.

Activity 2.5 ....

Mr Green wished to make a will, and on 17 July instructed a solicitor to prepare a will leaving £9,000 each to his two daughters. Nothing was done, however, until the managing clerk of the solicitors' firm arranged to visit Mr Green on 17 September. Unfortunately, Mr Green had been taken ill suddenly and had died on 14 September.

Do Mr Green's daughters have a claim for negligence against their father's solicitor?

Feedback ....

These are basically the facts of *White v Jones* [1995] 1 All ER 691. The House of Lords applied the 'assumption of responsibility' criterion to establish that a professional adviser owed a duty of care to a third party in circumstances where not to do so would result in an injustice. This case also extended the situations in which a 'special relationship' (see the *Hedley Byrne* case discussed above) may be said to exist to include those between a professional adviser and those intended to benefit from the task accepted by the professional adviser. In this case, Mr. Green's daughters would have a claim for negligence against their father's solicitor.

Summary

In this session you have learned about the concept of tort and, especially, the tort of negligence and the essential elements of duty, breach of duty, damage, loss, injury and liability in a business context. You have also learned that the importance of negligence is relevant to professional advisers. They may have to account for the consequences of it in financial statements for clients, as in tort, by way of provisions and so on, but also may face a charge of negligence themselves if they are careless in providing advice or in auditing financial statements. Indeed, in recent years, financial cases have been influential in developing case law in the area of negligence. From the law of tort and negligence, Session 3 goes on to consider the law of contract as another major area of business law.

SESSION **3 The law of contract**

Introduction

Upon completion of Session 3 you are expected to be able to:

- identify the elements of a valid contract and the required forms of contract in specific circumstances
- understand enforceable offers and acceptances, issues concerning communications and the role of consideration
- explain the principles for establishing parties' intention that an agreement has contractual force and the impact of misrepresentation
- understand 'express' and 'implied' contract terms, also conditions and warranties
- understand the main provisions of legislation relating to the sale of goods and supply of services, including the use of exclusion clauses and unfair terms in consumer and non-consumer transactions
- explain what is meant by 'performance' (and the level required to fulfil contractual obligations); by 'non-performance' (including valid reasons, breach by the other party and frustration); and by 'remedies' (specific performance, rescission, etc.)
- understand issues relating to damages, for example, remoteness and quantification.

Firms make contracts all the time in furtherance of their business, so an understanding of contract law is important. Like tort, contract law is applicable internationally, although in the discussions that follow we refer to the English system to provide examples and illustrations. It is obvious that business deals will have financial effects, as this is how businesses make profits. Accountants therefore need to know how to deal with the financial outcomes of contracts. Things such as when payment is due, when 'title to goods' passes to a customer, what a client's liability is in terms of warranty for defective goods, etc., are all likely to have been specifically dealt with in business contracts and have the potential to affect financial statements, as Session 3 will illustrate.

3.1 **What is a contract?**

A contract is a legally binding agreement. It is essentially a deal that is enforceable at law. There are different types of contract. A valid contract is fully enforceable, whilst various other contracts are not. These different types of contract are discussed below.

- Valid contracts. These can be legally enforced in full. As you will learn in Section 3.2, there are several requirements which must be present for a valid contract to exist. If they are not present, then the contract will be impaired in some way, for which there is a variety of possible remedies. These remedies will also be covered in Session 3.

- Void contracts. These have no legal effect and no rights and duties arise. An example would be a contract for an illegal purpose, such as to steal something. Also, some contracts may be void if they are so uncertain that no one can determine what has been agreed.

- Voidable contracts. These will have legal effect unless one party sets it aside, which may happen if the contract was entered into based on a misrepresentation (see Section 3.2.6). The usual way of setting aside a contract is rescission, although there are limits on the right to rescission, as it is only possible if both parties can be restored to their original positions pre-contract.

- Unenforceable contracts. These have legal effect but cannot be enforced. Examples might be where contract is of a type that has to be evidenced in writing, but has not been, so while valid, cannot be enforced, or where a contract is contrary to public policy.

The common law doctrine of privity of contract established that only parties to a contract could sue or be sued under that contract. However, the *Contract (Rights of Third Parties) Act 1999* provides that a person who is not a party to a contract may in his/her own right enforce a term of a contract if:

- the contract expressly permits it; or

- a term of the contract confers a benefit on a third party and the contract cannot be construed as excluding the right of that third party to enforce the contract.

Contracts do not necessarily have to be in writing: many are oral. It may, however, be desirable to have a written agreement for the purpose of proving what was agreed, but it is not necessary for legal validity. Exceptionally, some contracts must be in writing to be legally valid. These are discussed below.

- Bills of exchange, promissory notes, cheques, contracts of marine insurance, transfers of shares in a company and legal assignment of debts will be void if not in writing.

- Hire purchase and other regulated consumer credit agreements may be unenforceable against a borrower unless they are made in writing and contain information as required by the *Consumer Credit Act 1974*. Contracts of guarantee do not have to be in writing, but are unenforceable in court unless the essential terms are evidenced in writing and unless they are signed by or on behalf of the guarantor.

- Contracts to sell or lease land must be in writing under the *Law of Property (Miscellaneous Provisions) Act 1989* and must contain all the terms expressly agreed by the parties, which they must sign. (This does not apply where land is sold by public auction.) There is a second stage required to complete the transaction, however, whereby the title of the land is legally conveyed to the purchaser in return for payment (or the remainder of the payment if a deposit has been made at the first stage when the sale/lease contract is signed). This conveyance must be by a document known as a deed if the land is sold, or leased for more than three years. A deed is a formal document which must be signed and the signature witnessed formally (that is, an independent person must sign to acknowledge he/she has seen this signing take place). Formal **delivery** must also take place. ('Delivery' here means that there should be an intention to put the deed into effect, rather than physically handing anything over.) Deeds are required to ensure the legal validity of promises which are made without **consideration** and for some bills of sale (**mortgages of goods**).

Activity 3.1 ....

Mr Hokka hired for three months a commercial oven, which he intended to use in the manufacture of illegal drugs. Ms Piper, from whom he hired it, did not know the exact nature of his proposed use, but was aware that it was illegal. After paying one month's instalment, Mr Hokka returned the oven. Ms Piper wishes to know if she can sue Mr Hokka for damages for breaching his contract.

Feedback ....

Although the contract of hire appears valid, it will actually be void owing to illegality, as the drugs being manufactured are illegal, and both parties know of the intention to use the oven for an illegal purpose, even if Ms Piper did not know the specific illegality involved. Ms Piper therefore cannot sue for damages. If she had not known of the illegal purpose and had not been implicated in the illegality, she would have been able to sue.

3.2 Obligations imposed by a contract

The basic requirements of a contract are listed below and then discussed in detail:

- offer and acceptance of that offer (= agreement)
- contractual capacity
- consideration
- intention to create legal relations
- absence of vitiating factors.

3.2.1 Offer and acceptance of that offer

A contract is formed after an offer has been accepted. An offer is an undertaking by the offeror (the person who makes the offer) to be contractually bound by the terms of his or her offer. An acceptance must be an absolute and unqualified acceptance of the offer as it stands, including any terms attached to it. Where the offer and acceptance are both promises, the contract is **bilateral**. Where the offer is a promise and the acceptance is an act, the contract is **unilateral**. For example, if a tutor promises to give a box of chocolates to the first student who gets the correct answer to a question, this is an offer. The acceptance by a student would be that student getting the first right answer and claiming the box of chocolates. The acceptance is via an act, so would be a unilateral contract.

An offer can be to the world at large. For example, in the case of *Carlill v Carbolic Smoke Ball Co* [1893] 1 QB 256, via the following newspaper advertisement, the company stated that it would pay £100 to anyone who became ill with influenza after using its 'smoke ball' as directed, and that to show that the offer was genuine, it had deposited £1,000 in a bank account. Mrs Carlill used the 'smoke ball', but caught influenza nonetheless. It was held that the advertisement was an offer (to the world) which Mrs Carlill accepted when she used the 'smoke ball' as directed, and that Mrs Carlill was entitled to the £100. (This was a unilateral contract.)

Carbolic smoke ball advertisement

Offers must be distinguished from other actions which appear to be similar. An invitation to treat is an invitation to make an offer. It is an indication that a person is willing to enter into or continue negotiations, but is not yet willing to be bound by the terms mentioned. Advertisements of goods for sale in newspapers or catalogues, goods displayed in a shop window, shares in a company prospectus, and invitations to tender for the supply of goods or services, are usually therefore invitations to treat. The other party is being invited to make an offer, which may then be accepted or refused. Remember that a shopkeeper is not obliged to sell you any goods if he/she does not wish to accept your offer to buy them: he/she will merely be declining your offer. In a self-service store, goods displayed on shelves are also an invitation to treat (*Pharmaceutical Society of Great Britain v Boots Cash Chemists* [1953] 2 WLR 427).

Advertisements as invitations to treat must also be distinguished from sales 'puff' or boasts (which claim that a product is, for example, the 'best in town'), as these can sometimes seem like promises or offers, and also from declarations of intention. In *Harris v Nickerson* (1873) LR 8 QB 286, the defendant auctioneer advertised office furniture for sale, but the furniture was withdrawn. The claimant, who had attended the auction intending to buy the furniture, claimed that the advertisement amounted to an offer to sell which he accepted by attending the auction. It was held that this was not an offer to sell: the bid would have been the offer which the auctioneer could then accept or reject.

There are further rules about offers.

- They must be communicated. Until one party knows of the offer by another, he/she cannot accept it. For example, a person who hands back lost property not knowing that a reward has been offered is not entitled to claim the reward.

- Offers lapse on expiry of a prescribed time or after a reasonable period (which will depend upon particular circumstances), also on the death of either party before acceptance. An offer will lapse as well if it is conditional upon other criteria and these are not fulfilled. For example, an offer to buy goods assumes that the goods will remain in the same state and not be damaged before they are purchased.

- Revocation (withdrawal of an offer) is permissible as long as there has been no acceptance, and provided that the revocation has been communicated to the offeree (the person to whom the offer was made). Revocation may be expressly made or implied by other conduct (e.g., selling goods elsewhere), and communication may be direct or through another reliable source. In *Dickinson v Dodds* (1875–76) LR 2 ChD 463, the offeree heard through a friend that a house that had been offered for sale had been sold elsewhere. However, this means of communication has been criticised for lack of certainty. An offer can be revoked at any time before acceptance, even if there has been a promise to keep the offer open for a specified period. However, if an option has been bought (i.e., the other party has provided consideration to keep the offer open for a period of time), then a subsidiary contract has been formed in respect of the time period, and an early withdrawal of the offer will breach this subsidiary contract.

- The offer terminates if the offeree rejects it, provided that the rejection is communicated to the offeror, or if the offeree makes a counter-offer or accepts it subject to new terms. In *Hyde v Wrench* (1840) 49 All ER Rep 132, the defendant offered to sell his farm to the claimant for £1,000. The claimant responded by offering to buy it for £950, but the defendant refused to sell. The claimant then tried to accept the original offer to sell for £1,000, but could not do so as his counter-offer of £950 had terminated the original offer. However, a request for information in response to an offer is not a rejection and counter-offer, and the offeror can, of course, accept a counter-offer or new terms proposed if he/she chooses to do so.

- Where an offer is made to a group of persons and one of them accepts, that offer then ceases to exist as far as the remainder of the group is concerned. This is because the acceptance by one group member terminates the offer made to the others. If it did not, in practical terms, this could cause chaos.

Activity 3.2 ···

What is the status of these responses to an offer by Joe to sell a car to Rashid at £3,000, and what are the legal effects?

(a) Rashid says 'Yes, I'll buy at £3,000'.

(b) Rashid says 'I'll give you £2,750'.

(c) Rashid asks if Joe would be willing to consider £2,750.

(d) Rashid says 'Yes, I'll buy at £3,000 payable in two instalments'.

Feedback

(a) Rashid says 'Yes, I'll buy at £3,000'. Acceptance.

(b) Rashid says 'I'll give you £2,750'. Counter-offer, therefore the offer terminates.

(c) Rashid asks if Joe would be willing to consider £2,750. This looks like an enquiry, so the offer would remain open to be accepted on the original terms if Joe said 'no'.

(d) Rashid says 'Yes, I'll buy at £3,000 payable in two instalments'. This looks like an acceptance subject to new terms (the original offer does not mention payment by instalment), so the offer would terminate.

In (b) and (d), Joe could, of course, decide to accept the counter-offer or the new terms, but this would then put Rashid in the position of being the offeror.

Sometimes an acceptance may be made 'subject to a written agreement' or 'subject to contract'.

It will then need to be decided whether the parties intended to be bound immediately (with the later document being just a record of this), or whether there is no intention to be bound until a written agreement should be produced. If an agreement is of the type that will not be valid unless made in writing, then the latter must apply. Care must be exercised about documents which are described as 'letters of intent' or 'heads of agreement', as, although prima facie, they are not binding, this may be contradicted by the actual wording if it is sufficiently definite.

Where parties negotiate a contract, it is common for them each to have their own 'standard terms and conditions'. From the actual content of these terms and conditions, it can be extremely difficult to determine a binding contract, as the terms and conditions of the parties are different from each other. This situation is commonly referred to as a 'battle of the forms'. If one party carries out obligations under the agreement, in general he/she will be deemed to have accepted the other party's terms and conditions, and the contract would proceed on that basis.

3.2.2   More about acceptance

As acceptance completes a contract, the place where acceptance occurs is the place of the contract. This is important in the case of parties negotiating in different countries, as it may determine, if it is not specified in the contract, which country's laws will apply.

With exceptions, actual communication is necessary for acceptance to be valid. Silence, therefore, does not indicate acceptance, even where, following an offer, the seller says that 'if he hears nothing to the contrary, he will assume that the item is bought'. This happened in the case of a horse offered for sale in *Felthouse v Brindley* (1862) 6 LT 157.

Note that in the case of unsolicited goods (sent by post with a note saying that if they are not returned within a specified period, the recipient will be bound to pay for them), under the *Unsolicited Goods and Services Act 1971*, the recipient is not bound to pay unless he/she treats the goods as his/her own by using them or intentionally destroys them.

Dear Company:
I'm not interested in your product.

Signed,
Occupant

There are two exceptions to the rule that actual communication is required. The first exception is in a unilateral offer (as in *Carlill*), where action is enough to indicate acceptance. The second is when the 'postal rule' applies. For acceptance by post, the time of posting is the time of acceptance, even if the letter does not arrive (established in *Adams v Lindsell* (1818) 1 B & Aid 680, and *Household Fire Insurance & Carriage Accident Insurance Co Ltd v Grant* (1878–79) LR 4 ExD 216). The postal rule can be excluded if there is a specific requirement actually to give notice of acceptance (*Holwell Securities v Hughes* [1974] 1 WLR 155). The postal rule only applies where it is contemplated by the parties that the post will be used, for example, if previous negotiations had taken place by post. There must also be evidence of posting in the normal way. It is not enough to hand a letter to someone to post, or even to a postman. For other, more instantaneous forms of communication (telephone, fax, or telex, though fax and telex are less frequently used these days), acceptance is effective when and where it reaches the other party (*Entores v Miles Far Eastern Corporation* [1955] 3 WLR 48). It is less certain how the postal rules apply to e-mail communications, and although there are now regulations that relate to electronic commerce

(*Electronic Commerce (EC Directive) Regulations 2002*), it is not absolutely clear when an e-mail is considered delivered – when sent, when it arrives in the recipient's mail box or when it is read. Some cases have already reached the courts on this issue, and it seems likely that there will be more. This is an area where law is evolving.

3.2.3 Contractual capacity

To enter into a contract, a person must have legal capacity to do so. For example, a minor (a person aged under 18, often also referred to as a 'child' or an 'infant') has a limited power to contract. This limitation is designed to protect minors from exploitation by adults. However, contracts for the sale of necessary goods (i.e., things a person needs to live) that are sold and actually delivered to a minor are valid under common law and binding upon him/her, although other contracts (e.g., for the sale or purchase of land, etc.) are voidable. Someone who suffers from a mental disorder also has limited power to contract. Some local authorities have limited contractual capacity as they can only carry out activities for which they were created or which they have special authority to do. All else is beyond their legal power (*ultra vires*).

3.2.4 Consideration

A contract is in the nature of a bargain, whereby one party promises to do something (e.g., sell goods) in return for something done by the other party (e.g., pay for the goods). The promised payment is known as consideration for the goods (and vice versa). Consideration does not have to be goods or money. It may take the form of an act, forbearance to act or a promise. If a promise will be fulfilled in the future, it is known as executory consideration. When it is eventually fulfilled it is called executed consideration.

The classic definition is regarded as that of Lush, J:

> A valuable consideration, in the sense of the law, may consist either in some right, interest, profit or benefit accruing to the one party, or some forbearance, detriment, loss or responsibility given, suffered or undertaken by the other.
>
> *Currie v Misa* (1875) LR 10 Ex 153, at 162

Pre-contract or past consideration (i.e., prior to the contract being agreed) is not valid consideration because it is not part of the contractual promise and therefore has no value. However, if work is undertaken, and it is the type of work that is normally paid for, then it may be implied from the outset that everyone intended that the work would be paid for. For example, if a plumber is asked to do repairs, does the work and sends his bill afterwards, then there is an implied promise to pay by the recipient of the services, which would be binding. The work done in these circumstances is not past consideration.

There must always be some consideration for a contract to be valid, but it does not have to match (in terms of value) the consideration given by the other party. Thus, consideration could be a nominal sum, say £1. Note that a deed will be required to enforce the legal validity of promises which are made without consideration (see Section 3.1).

A promise to perform an existing obligation similarly has no value, as the promisor is already bound by the promise or existing contract made. For instance, if a debtor promises to pay part of his/her debt in consideration of the creditor releasing him/her from the rest, the release is not binding. This follows the rule established in *Pinnel's case* (1602) 5 Co Rep 117a, which has been the basis of all subsequent applications and interpretations of the law.

The term 'approved' in this context means that a later case follows the principles established by an earlier case as valid law.

In *Foakes v Beer* (1883–4) LR 9 App Cas 605, which approved *Pinnel*, the issue was whether Dr Foakes owed interest on a debt to Mrs Beer. The latter was entitled to receive interest on the debt as it was a judgment debt (Mrs Beer had sued him to recover her money), but she subsequently entered into an agreement with Dr Foakes, drawn up by his solicitor, whereby he was allowed to pay the £2,090 19s[3] owed by a sum of £500 on the signing of the agreement and the rest by instalments. Dr Foakes repaid the £2,090 19s, but paid no interest. In 1882 Mrs Beer sought to recover this interest. Dr Foakes was initially successful at trial in his contention that she had foregone the right to interest, though the Court of Appeal reversed this. On appeal to the House of Lords, Mrs Beer was successful. There was no additional consideration provided by him for her foregoing interest on the debt.

However, one might consider that to some extent there is a kind of practical benefit implicit as a type of consideration: Mrs Beer did not have further recourse to the court on the issue and she did receive some money (Dr Foakes might have defaulted altogether). This idea of practical or subjective benefit (as opposed to objective benefit measurable in monetary terms), has been raised in subsequent cases, although some have followed *Foakes* outright (e.g., *Re Selectmove* [1995] 1 WLR 474 and *D. & C. Builders v Rees* [1966] 2 QB 617).

A notable case is *Stilk v Myrick* (1809) 2 Camp 317 and 6 Esp 129. Stilk, a seaman, agreed with the captain of his ship to work the ship back to London after two of the eleven crew members deserted. He and the remaining crew would share the deserters' wages between them. The captain refused to pay, and Stilk sued: he did not succeed. The case was reported by two different reporters who each give a different reason for his failure. One suggests that the failure was on the grounds of public policy to prevent the possibility of sailors at sea extorting money from their captains for performing their contractual duty. The other suggests that Stilk failed because he had not provided consideration in return for the captain's promise as he was only doing what he was obliged to do. From a twenty-first century perspective it seems difficult to defend the latter decision, as Stilk seemed to provide consideration by doing extra work, although it is possible to infer that the crew's contract would include covering for desertion as an occupational hazard, given the nature of the work. This case does not sit easily with a decision in *Hartley v Ponsonby* (1857) 7 El & Bl 872 where facts were similar, other than that 17 out of 36 crew members deserted. Here it was held that the original contract was terminated because it was dangerous to sail a ship with

[3] The sum is expressed in 'old' money pre-decimalisation. A 'shilling' denoted by 's', was one twentieth of a pound (five pence in current money) and contained 12 old pence (or 'pennies').

19 men, and a new contract was formed for which good consideration was provided.

The idea of practical benefit in terms of performing an existing duty was considerably advanced in the 1990 case of *Williams v Roffey Bros & Nicholls (Contractors) Ltd* [1991] 1 QB 1. Here a carpenter, Williams, sub-contracted for part of the refurbishment of a block of flats, ran into financial difficulties such that the job would not have been completed in time for the original contractors to avoid a financial penalty. It was agreed to pay an additional sum per flat (now to be completed one at a time) to Williams to ensure that the work was done on time. The contractors then refused to pay. It was held that Williams was entitled to the additional sum on the grounds that the practical benefits gained by the contractors constituted consideration: (i) the sub-contractor could continue with his work and did not breach his contract; (ii) the defendants were spared the trouble of hiring another sub-contractor; (iii) the work was done on time and the financial penalty avoided; (iv) the formal payment structure facilitated better financial control; and (v) the completion of one flat at a time enabled other tradesmen to do their work in the flats, which otherwise would have been delayed.

Some earlier cases suggest another possible limit to the consideration rules. Although a promise without consideration cannot be sued on, it can sometimes be used in a defence known as promissory estoppel (a remedy provided in equity, rather than common law), as exemplified in the case of *Central London Property Trust Ltd v High Trees House Ltd* [1947] 1 KB 130. In the *High Trees* case, landlords were effectively prevented from going back on a deal they had made for which they had received no consideration, because it would have been unfair to allow them to do so. The landlords had promised to accept lower rent from sub-let flats which had become difficult to rent out in the 1940s in war-torn London. When they tried later to reclaim retrospectively the higher rent for the wartime period, the judge, Lord Denning, invoking equitable principles, ruled that they could collect the higher rent with effect from the end of the war (peace-time conditions being re-established), but were estopped (prevented) from collecting it in arrears in respect of the wartime period. The case has caused much comment. The general feeling seems to be that while the sub-letters could not have sued on the landlords' promise because they had not provided consideration for it, the landlords were prevented from doing so, because they themselves had acted in accordance with it. This defence may apply to fewer cases, given the verdict in *Williams v Roffey*.

A promise to perform an existing public duty will also not normally be valid consideration, as it would be contrary to public policy. However, if the promise is to do more than the public duty (e.g., provide extra police officers to perform guard duty if there is public unrest), this will be sufficient consideration. Note, however, that a promise to perform an existing obligation to a third party can be consideration (e.g., in a situation where Z promises X a guarantee if X promises Z that he will pay an existing debt to Y).

Activity 3.3 ··

Jennifer is a student at a private, fee-paying university. Because of the collapse of her parents' business in the economic downturn, she is no longer able to pay her fees. The university is keen for Jennifer to remain with them, and reduces her fees. Six months later, Jennifer inherits £5 million when a distant relative unexpectedly dies. The university puts her fees back up to their former level and asks her to refund the amount by which the fees had been reduced in the last six months.

Does the university have the right to do this? Advise Jennifer.

Feedback ··

The first question to consider is the nature of the fee reduction. While it is impossible to be definite about this, it does seem to be the case that the university has waived its contractual rights. (A **waiver** is the act of abandoning, or refraining to assert, a legal right.) However, it could be the case that there has been a new contract or the terms of the old one have been varied (see Section 3.3.4).

If the fee reduction is a waiver in response to Jennifer's changed personal circumstances, the university can restore the full fee once the problem has been eliminated. However, the doctrine of promissory estoppel (see *Central London Property Trust Ltd v High Trees House Ltd* discussed earlier), would mean that the university would be prevented from recovering the amount by which the fees had been reduced for the six month period in question. In equity, a promise that has been relied on can be enforced without consideration. In this instance there has been no consideration as Jennifer has not done anything in exchange for the university reducing its fees.

However, an alternative approach here would be to apply *Williams v Roffey*. Consideration for a variation in contract terms may have been the practical benefit that the university gained in not losing all of Jennifer's fees. Either way, Jennifer would appear to have a good case to prevent the university trying to reclaim the reduction applied in the six month period.

This is a good example of there being two different legal ways to develop a solution to a legal problem.

3.2.5 Intention to create legal relations

The intention to create legal relations is presumed to exist in a business context, but presumed to be absent from a social context. For instance, an arrangement between friends to meet for a meal would not be a legally binding contract; and arrangements between married couples are not usually legal contracts, unless the couple is separated.

3.2.6 Absence of vitiating factors

A contract must not contain anything that makes it void, voidable or unenforceable. Vitiating factors (i.e., factors that impair the legal validity) are:

- mistake
- misrepresentation
- illegality
- duress
- undue influence.

These will be discussed below.

Mistake

There is no general legal doctrine of mistake, and rules that there are emerge from a variety of cases. Different terminology is used to describe various types of mistake.

- An identical (bilateral or common) mistake is where both parties make the same mistake about a fundamental fact, for example, about the actual existence of the subject matter.

- A mutual mistake is where the parties each make a different mistake and are at cross-purposes.

- A unilateral mistake is where one party is aware that the other has made a mistake, which may be in regard to contract terms or to the worth or value of the contract.

Depending on the severity and nature of the mistake, the contract may be void, voidable or may remain valid: it will depend on the circumstances. Sometimes a mistake can be rectified, especially if it is the case that a written term does not reflect the true nature of the agreement and this nature is not disputed by the parties.

Misrepresentation

A representation is a statement of fact by the representor inducing the representee to enter into a contract. It must be a statement of some specific, existing and verifiable fact or past event. A misrepresentation, on the other hand, is an untrue statement of fact, made with a view to inducing another party to enter into a contract. Normally excluded from the concept of representation (and therefore misrepresentation) are statements of law, future conduct or intention, opinion, sales 'puff' (hype), and advertising.

Silence is not generally considered a misrepresentation, as there is no duty to disclose facts, even if the silent party knows that the other party is deceiving himself/herself. In contracts for the sale of goods, this rule is known as *caveat emptor* (Latin for 'let the buyer beware'). However, there are exceptions, as follows.

1 A change of circumstances. There is a duty to correct statements which were true when made, but which, because facts have changed, have subsequently become false, and it would be unfair to let them stand. In *With v O'Flanagan* [1936] 1 All ER 727, negotiations took place between the claimant and the defendant, a doctor, for the sale of the latter's medical practice said to be worth £2,000. Four months later, a contract of sale was entered into, by which time the practice had become worthless because of the defendant's intervening illness. It was held that the defendant ought to have communicated this change of circumstance to the claimant.

2 A partial or half truth can be a misrepresentation. In *London Assurance v Mansel* (1879) LR 11 ChD 363, a person completing a life assurance application said that he had had two proposals accepted, but omitted to mention that several other applications had been rejected.

3 Where contracts are *uberrimae fidei* (Latin for 'of the utmost good faith'), that is, where one party alone possesses full knowledge of the material facts, that party must disclose them. This applies to contracts of insurance, contracts for the sale of land, share prospectuses and contracts for family arrangements.

4 Where there is a special relationship between parties to a contract, of a confidential or fiduciary nature, such as between principal and agent, then full disclosure of all material facts is required.

Types of misrepresentation

There are three types of misrepresentation.

1 Wholly innocent, where a party makes a statement in the genuine belief that it is true, based on reasonable grounds, but it turns out to be false.

2 Negligent, where a statement is made without having reasonable grounds for knowing whether it is true, though the maker of the statement might genuinely believe it to be true.

3 Fraudulent, where a party makes a statement knowing that it is false **or** without belief in its truth **or** recklessly (i.e., he/she is careless as to whether the statement is true or false).

The *Misrepresentation Act 1967* deals with wholly innocent and negligent misrepresentation but not fraudulent misrepresentation. If an allegation of negligence is made, the onus is on the representor to show reasonable grounds for belief (*s.2(1)*).

Forms of action and remedies

For fraudulent misrepresentation, an action will be brought in tort for damages for deceit and rescission (see Section 3.1) of the contract.

For negligent misrepresentation, an action will be brought in tort for damages for negligence (if *Hedley Byrne v Heller* principles apply (see Section 2.5)) or an action for damages under the 1967 Act. The burden of proof under the *Misrepresentation Act 1967* lies with the defendant; in the common law tort of negligence, the burden is with the claimant. Also, rescission of contract may be granted.

For wholly innocent misrepresentation, rescission is the usual remedy. The underlying idea is that as there is no fault by the defendant, no damages are necessary. However, a court has the discretion to substitute damages for rescission under *s.2(2)* of the *Misrepresentation Act*.

Rescission cannot be granted as a remedy if a party has affirmed a contract, that is, has treated the contract as continuing in existence, instead of exercising a right to rescind it for misrepresentation. Similarly, if full restitution of any property/goods transferred cannot be made, or if third party rights have accrued under the contract which must be protected, then rescission will not be possible. An order for rescission may be accompanied by an order for an indemnity to reimburse the claimant for obligations created by the contract, although this will not apply where damages are paid.

Illegality

Illegality is a vitiating factor. There are two aspects to this.

1   Illegal purpose. This has been referred to in Section 3.1. Certain kinds of contracts are forbidden by law, and will be void *ab initio* (Latin for 'from the beginning'), such as a contract to commit a crime. Others will be invalid because they are unenforceable owing to their purpose being contrary to public policy, such as engaging in immoral activity.

2   Illegal performance. The purpose of a contract may be legal, but the contract may be carried out in an illegal way. An example of this would be an employment contract (legal) where part of the income was not declared for income tax purposes (illegal). An innocent party in these circumstances would have the right to sue on the contract.

Duress

Where a party was improperly forced to enter into a contract, then the contract will be voidable by the innocent party. Duress may be a physical threat. An example might be where a person is forced to sell his/her house because of a threat of violence to him/her or respective family if he/she did not agree to the sale. It could also be non-physical, for example, economic duress. Duress is something more than 'hard bargaining'. In *Universe Tankships of Monrovia v International Transport Workers Federation (The Universe Sentinel)* [1982] 2 WLR 803, trade union officials threatened to induce the crew of a ship to break their contract of employment so as to prevent the ship leaving port unless the claimant made payments to the defendant's welfare fund. This would have had disastrous financial consequences for the ship owners. This was held to be economic duress.

Note that where cases involve ships, it is common to find the name of the ship as here (The Universe Sentinel), attached as part of the case name.

Undue influence

This occurs where someone has been persuaded or coerced into entering into a contract, or where someone was not able to make an independent decision, such that the contract can become voidable at the instigation of the innocent party. An example might be an elderly person being coerced into agreeing to repair work to his/her house which was not strictly needed. A presumption of undue influence is made in certain relationships such as doctor/patient, lawyer/client or parent/child relationships. In such circumstances, the weaker party should be given independent advice otherwise the contract is voidable by him/her. The issue of undue influence can arise between lender and borrower. Generally speaking, while a presumption of undue influence is not made, if a lender has information that a borrower is acting under the undue influence of another, then the borrower will be able to set aside the transaction.

The concepts of duress and undue influence must be distinguished from that of an **unconscionable (or catching) bargain**, which is a contract made on very unfair terms. There is no question of duress or undue influence here, but, rather, the principle is that of inequality of bargaining power. A person might enter into such a bargain simply because of a desperate need for money. Such a contract may be set aside or modified by a court empowered to grant equitable remedies.

Activity 3.4 ....

Consider the cartoon below.

'I gotta admit, he's one hell of a negotiator.'

Assuming that a contract has been negotiated and agreed with each individual, what do you think are the implications of the above situation?

Feedback ....

The two gentlemen in the cartoon seem to have been 'negotiated' out of all their clothes (apart from their underwear and socks), which might have been given as consideration for the other party's promise to each of them. The caption might indicate no more than admiration for another party's hard bargaining technique. On the other hand, given that loss of clothes implies a certain loss of dignity and is unusual, the cartoon might suggest that the contracts have been made on very unfair terms (unconscionable bargains), where the other party had considerably superior bargaining power. If such contracts are indicated, they could be set aside by a court empowered to grant equitable remedies.

It is not inconceivable that duress may be involved here, if the two gentlemen were compelled by some sort of threat to give up their clothes, or there might have been some form of undue influence. If either were the case, the contract would be voidable.

Again, this activity is characterised more by what we do not know than what we do, rather like Activity 1.1, which shows just how careful you have to be when interpreting facts and proposing possible legal solutions.

3.3 Contract terms

In this section, we turn to look at the rules governing contract terms. Terms must be certain, otherwise a contract will be void for uncertainty, and for some types of contracts the terms may need to be expressed in writing (see Section 3.1).

3.3.1 Types of contract terms

There are three types of contract terms, as discussed below.

1 **Express terms.** These are terms specifically mentioned and agreed to by the parties at the time of making the contract, in writing, orally or by a mixture of both.

2   Implied terms. These are terms which are implied in order to fill omissions and give business effect to the intentions of the parties. There are two types of implied terms, namely specific and generic.

Specific terms. These are implied in a particular contract (e.g., between X and Y) of a particular sort, to make it work, and are the type of terms which the parties would have agreed to had they considered the matter. For example, in *The Moorcock* [1886–1890] All ER Rep 530, where the owner of a wharf agreed to provide a berth for a ship, it was implied that the berth would be suitable.

Generic terms. These are terms implied into all contracts of a particular type, for example, contracts of sale or contracts of employment.

3   Statutory terms. These are terms which may be imposed by statute. This may occur as a result of codification of former (common) law, for example, implied terms in the contract of sale in the *Sale of Goods Act 1979*, or as a new legal initiative.

3.3.2   Incorporation of contract terms

Incorporation is a process by which terms from outside the contract are included in the contract. To be bound by a term, a person must know of that term or have been given reasonable notice of it when the contract was entered into.

Express terms may be incorporated by the following.

- Actual notice, where terms are known and agreed to by the parties at the time when the contract is entered into.

- Signature, where, if a person signs a document, he/she is prima facie deemed to have read the document and been given notice of the terms (*L'Estrange v Graucob Ltd* [1934] 2 KB 394).

- Provision of reasonable notice, such as where a hotel has a notice saying that its proprietors will not be held liable for the loss of articles left in the rooms. This notice will be effective if drawn to the guests' notice at the time they register (*Olley v Marlborough Court Ltd* 1 [1949] KB 532).

- Statute, irrespective of the express wishes of the contracting parties (see above). The *Sale of Goods Act 1979* (as amended in 1994) provides several examples of terms incorporated/implied by statute into every contract of sale, and these impose the following obligations on a seller:
  - that the seller has or will have the right to sell the goods
  - that the goods will correspond with any description applied to them
  - that the bulk will correspond with any sample
  - where the sale is made in the course of business, that the goods shall be both of satisfactory (formerly 'merchantable') quality and reasonably fit for the required purpose if the seller has been made aware of this.

The *Sale and Supply of Goods to Consumers Regulations 2002* (which came into effect on 31 March 2003) have introduced a number of amendments to the above *Sale of Goods Act* provisions. For example, in determining whether goods are of satisfactory quality, the buyer is entitled to take account of public statements (such as advertisements or labelling) made about the qualities of the goods. If goods prove defective, the buyer is entitled to repair, replacement, reduction in price or rescission up to six months after delivery, sometimes longer if circumstances warrant it.

These statutory rules have incorporated many common law case precedents. The *Sale of Goods Act* also imposes other duties. For example, payment for goods becomes due on delivery and the buyer is entitled to delivery of all the goods at once. These terms apply only if the parties have not varied them to allow the buyer credit or to allow delivery by instalments.

The *Supply of Goods and Services Act 1982* applies to contracts which are mainly for services, but in the course of which some goods are provided. It imposes obligations as regards materials that are almost the same as the *Sale of Goods Act*. In terms of service, there is a wider statutory requirement for the supplier to carry out the service with reasonable care and skill.

3.3.3 Status of contract terms

The terms of a contract can be categorised into the following.

- Conditions. A condition is a term of such importance that, if it is not adhered to, then the whole purpose of the contract is threatened. If a condition is breached, it does not automatically cause the contract to be terminated, but it will give the innocent party a choice of how to proceed. He/she may repudiate (cancel) the contract and claim damages and rescission, or he/she may choose to affirm (carry on with) the contract and claim damages. In general, conditions in a contract are regarded as supreme.

- Warranties. A warranty is less important than a condition. Failure to observe a warranty will not threaten the whole contract. An innocent party is not entitled to repudiate the contract but can claim for damages. If an innocent party should proceed by repudiating the contract following a breach of warranty, then that party will have acted in breach. In *Bettini v Gye* (1875–76) LR 1 QBD 183, the claimant was an opera singer and agreed to be present for rehearsals six days before the first performance at Covent Garden. He arrived three days late because of illness, but the defendant terminated his contract. It was held that the defendant was not entitled to do this as the claimant could still substantially perform his contract. Therefore, the agreement to be there six days before for rehearsals was a warranty and not a condition.

- Innominate terms. If it is not known whether a term is a warranty or a condition, it is said to be an innominate term. Lack of clear classification can create difficulties where there is a breach of a term the status of which is undecided. It is the nature and severity of a breach that determine its status (*Hong Kong Fir Shipping Co Ltd v Kawaski Kisen Kaisha Ltd* [1926] 2 QB 26).

In general, the law allows contracting parties the freedom to classify terms as they choose. However, if the status of terms is unclear, what may appear to one party as something of vital importance may seem to the other to be a minor consideration. The court will then have the difficult task of deciding what the parties' intentions were. There are some general guidelines. For example, if the law states that the term in question is a condition, then this is indisputable. If the contract states that breach of a particular term gives the innocent party the right to terminate, then that term will be a condition. A contract itself may describe a term as a condition or warranty. This is helpful, but not absolutely decisive, as the courts may come to a different view. If the innocent party has been deprived of what it was intended that he/she should receive under the contract, then there may be a breach of a condition, but this is regarded as a less certain test, as it looks at the outcome rather than the parties' intentions.

3.3.4   Variation of contract terms

It is possible for parties to vary the terms of their contract once it has been made. In making changes to contracts, the normal legal requirements of agreement and consideration must be met.

Some matters may be at the discretion of one of the parties. For example, in providing a service, the supplier may have a right to sub-contract. Also one party may reserve the right to vary terms unilaterally, for example, a loan with a variable interest rate. There would be an implied term of reasonable notice. If there is an agreed contractual change, it may be expressly agreed, implied from conduct (*Aparau v Iceland Frozen Foods plc (No. 2)* [2000] ICR 341) or agreed through incorporation.

Activity 3.5

The facts below are those of *Bannerman v White* (1861) 4 LT 740.

White, a hop merchant, was negotiating the purchase of hops from Bannerman. He asked Bannerman if any sulphur had been used in the treatment of the hops, saying that if it had, he would not even bother to ask the price. Bannerman said that no sulphur had been used. The negotiations led to a contract of sale. Later White discovered that sulphur was used in five out of the 300 acres on which the hops were grown, and refused to go ahead with the contract. Bannerman sued for the price of the sale.

How do you think the court decided?

Feedback

The statement that sulphur had not been used was held to be an express term of the contract. The claimant knew of the objection that hop merchants had to sulphured hops, and it was held that the contract was conditional on sulphur not having been used in the growth of the hops. If sulphur had been so used, the defendant was at liberty to reject the hops, so Bannerman had breached the contract and could not sue.

3.3.5   Unfair contract terms

Although it may be assumed that both parties in a contract are able to negotiate freely, in reality, this may not be possible as their bargaining positions may be very different. For example, one may be in a much stronger position than the other, because it is a monopoly or near-monopoly provider. One may be in a weaker position because of financial pressure or a lack of the technical knowledge required to assess the quality of complex technical goods. The possibility of genuine bargaining is severely diminished in such circumstances, and the weaker party often feels compelled to accept a standard form of terms and conditions, containing a lot of clauses in small print, which he/she does not really understand.

This situation may be open to abuse by the stronger party, who may attempt to include harsh penalties for a breach of any contract clauses which attempt to limit or exclude totally his/her own liability (**exemption/exclusion clauses**). Courts have been compelled to decide whether such clauses have been valid, and in certain instances there is now legislation to protect weaker parties, such as the *Unfair Contract Terms Act 1977*, which is discussed later.

Attitude of the courts to exemption clauses

Before it accepts an exemption clause as a valid contract term, the court must be satisfied that the party against whom the clause is being enforced genuinely agreed to it before or when the contract was made. If the contract is one made by signing a written document, the signatory will usually be bound by terms included even if he/she has not read them (*L'Estrange v Graucob Ltd* – see Section 3.3.2). If it is an unsigned document, then it must be proved that the other party knew or should have known that it was meant to be a contract, and that everything possible was done to ensure that he/she knew of the terms. Many cases have involved documents such as travel or parking tickets, and a problem of the actual location of the conditions under which the tickets have been issued (*Thompson v London Midland & Scottish Railway Co* [1929] All ER 474; *Thornton v Shoe Lane Parking Ltd* [1971] 2 WLR 585). If a party has not read a term, but every opportunity has been provided for him/her to do so, it is considered that **constructive communication** has been given.

'You didn't read the small print, sir – your ticket restricts you to a seat kicked continuously by a small child.'

As regards previous dealings, where the defendant has not given the claimant a copy of the conditions, or drawn attention to them when making the contract, the doctrine of constructive communication will not apply and so the defendant cannot rely on communications in previous dealings, unless those dealings have been frequent. This does not apply in any case in consumer transactions (where people buy for personal use).

An attempt to introduce an exemption clause after the contract has been made will be ineffective, as in the case of *Olley v Marlborough Court Ltd*, already referred to in Section 3.3.2. Similarly the courts have not permitted a party to misrepresent the effect of a contract term (*Curtis v Chemical Cleaning & Dyeing Co* [1951] 1 KB 805); enforce unduly burdensome clauses (*Interfoto Picture Library Ltd v Stiletto Visual Programmes Ltd* [1989] QB 433) or a clause that was inconsistent with a main contract term (*J. Evans & Son (Portsmouth) Ltd v Andrea Merzario Ltd* [1976] 2 All ER 930).

Where there are any ambiguities in exemption clauses, courts have usually decided against the party attempting to rely on them (*contra proferentem*), and will tend to look more favourably on clauses which limit liability (e.g., to a particular sum of money) rather than seek to exclude it completely. Courts will also apply the repugnancy rule. This means that where an exemption clause is in direct contradiction to the main purpose of the contract, it can be struck out. In *Pollock v Macrae* 1922 SC (HL) 192, in a contract to build and supply marine engines, the defendant firm included an exclusion clause designed to protect them from liability for defective workmanship and materials. The engines supplied were so defective that they could not be used. The House of Lords struck out the exemption clause as repugnant to the contract's main purpose, which was to build and supply workable engines. Courts will also enforce the four corners rule, whereby the exemption clause is only available provided that the contract is being performed in accordance with its terms (the 'four corners' of the contract). In *Thomas National Transport (Melbourne) Pty and Pay v May and Baker (Australia) Pty Ltd* [1966] 2 Lloyd's Rep 347, valuable goods were destroyed in a fire which occurred when they were stored overnight in a lorry at the home of a sub-contractor instead of at the main carrier's depot. While there was a fundamental contract breach (see later) involved here, the case is often regarded as an instance where the 'four corners' rule could have been applied.

Unfair Contract Terms Act 1977 (UCTA)

The 1977 Act is the most important statute affecting exemption clauses. It deals largely with liability arising from things done in the course of business or from the occupation of premises for business purposes. It does not cover certain types of contracts – those relating to land, insurance and the formation/management of companies.

Under the 1977 Act, business liability in contract or tort cannot be excluded for death or bodily injury arising from negligence. Liability for financial loss or loss of property arising from negligence can be excluded or limited if it is reasonable to do so, and an exemption clause can only be included in a standard form contract where a consumer is involved if it is reasonable. Consumers (people who buy for private use) are given special protection in contracts for the sale of goods by those who sell in the course of business. Implied terms as to title, description, sample, quality and fitness for purpose cannot be excluded, though they may be if the buyer is a non-consumer, and it is reasonable. Contracts of hire purchase, work, hire and for materials, along with various types of guarantees, are governed by similar rules.

The burden of proof for the *UCTA* test of reasonableness lies with the person claiming that the test is reasonable. Factors in applying the test include: consideration of the circumstances when the contract was made; the resources of the person relying on the clause and the opportunities for insurance, where there are limits on the amount payable; where the supply of goods took place; the bargaining position of the parties; the availability of other supplies; inducements to agree the clause; the buyer's knowledge of the extent of the clause; customs of the trade and previous dealings; and whether the goods were made, processed or adapted to the order of the buyer. In *R.W. Green Ltd v Cade Bros Farms* [1978] 1 Lloyd's Rep 602, it was held by the court as unreasonable to impose a time limit of three days for complaints. The goods in question were seed potatoes, in which flaws might not be apparent until after they had started to grow.

'Now this is the standard company contract – I want you to stick in a couple of loopholes.'

Unfair Terms in Consumer Contracts Regulations 1999

The 1999 regulations were implemented in response to an EU directive and are not limited to exemption clauses, but apply also to penalty clauses (whereby a person who breaks a contract term will be required to pay compensation) and to some inertia clauses (where obligations may be extended if a party forgets to act). However, unlike the *UCTA*, the *Regulations* only apply to consumer contracts (so not to companies, trade/professional partnerships, government departments or local authorities) and to standard contract terms (i.e., not individually negotiated ones). Employment contracts are specifically excluded, as are those in respect of incorporation and/or organisation of companies and partnerships, but the *Regulations* do cover insurance and mortgages of land.

The standard contract terms should be written in plain, easily understood language. Doubts about interpretation will be resolved in favour of the consumer, and any unfair term will not be binding. The *Regulations* give extensive, but not exhaustive, guidance on what is considered unfair. Unfairness is regarded as contrary to a requirement of good faith, as it causes an imbalance in the parties' rights and duties which operate to the consumer's detriment. An unfair term does not bind a consumer, but the contract may still be capable of continuance. A consumer may complain to the Office of Fair Trading, which may ask the supplier to discontinue the term or, if necessary, seek a court injunction.

Other relevant legislation

There is a variety of other legislation which imposes limits on contractual terms, on exemption clauses especially.

- The *Misrepresentation Act 1967* renders a term to exclude liability for misrepresentation voidable unless the exemption is fair and reasonable.

- The *Consumer Credit Act 1974* protects debtors during the period in which they owe money, as does the *Consumer Credit Act 2006*.

- The *Fair Trading Act 1973* allows the Department for Business, Innovation and Skills (formerly the Department of Trade and Industry) to issue delegated legislation to ban consumer trade practices if they are considered inappropriate.

3.4 Discharging (bringing to an end) a contract

Parties can be released from their contractual obligations in the following ways:

- agreement
- performance
- frustration
- breach.

We shall examine each of these in turn.

3.4.1 Agreement

Parties may have agreed when a contract can end. Sometimes it is implied that the parties have agreed that the contract can be ended, for example, in the case of an employment contract. Otherwise the parties need to enter a second contract to agree to end the first. If the first contract has not been performed at all, then this is straightforward as each party is providing consideration by giving up the other's obligation. Where the first contract has been partly or wholly performed then additional consideration is necessary, or release could be given in the form of a deed (of discharge).

3.4.2 Performance

This occurs when the exact performance of all the obligations of the contract have been completed and will discharge it. However, lesser performance will suffice in the following circumstances:

- where the contract is divisible, such as the building of a house, for which payment may be claimed at different stages as building progresses (e.g., laying the foundations, when the roof is put on, when the house is completed, etc.)
- where the contract can be fulfilled by substantial performance, such as the building of a house, where only minor matters are left outstanding
- where performance has been prevented by the other party, such as a plumber being denied access to a house
- where the contract is frustrated (see below).

If a contracting party is able to accept or reject partial performance of a contract, and chooses to accept, then a reasonable sum must be paid for the performance received on a *quantum meruit* basis (Latin for 'as much as he/she has earned/deserved').

3.4.3 Frustration

This occurs when:

- the sole subject matter of the contract has gone
- supervening changes in the law make the contract illegal
- the event which is the sole reason for the contract does not happen
- a party to the contract dies or becomes incapacitated.

Therefore, in general, a contract becomes frustrated if it becomes impossible, illegal or its commercial basis is destroyed. In the case of frustration, neither party may be at fault. In *Taylor v Caldwell* (1863) 3 Best and Smith 826, a music hall hired for a series of concerts was accidentally burnt down without the fault of either party. The hiring contract was thus frustrated.

At common law, frustration automatically brought the contract to an end. All monies previously paid were recoverable and sums not yet paid ceased to be payable. This could have very unfair results, as the case of *Fibrosa Spolka Akcyjna v Fairbairn Lawson Coombe Barbour Ltd* [1943] AC 32 shows. A contract by an English company to supply machinery to a Polish company was frustrated by the outbreak of World War II. The English company had already incurred costs in manufacturing the machinery, but was obliged to return money already received on account and was left without any claim on the Polish company. As a result, the *Law Reform (Frustrated Contracts) Act 1943* was passed. Although the common law rules still apply, by this Act, if a party had incurred expenses prior to formal discharge of the contract, the court has the discretion to allow that party to retain monies paid or recover all/part of further sums due, although the other party has a right of reclaim if the first party has received any valuable benefit other than money. This is rather like rescission, but with the court empowered to adjust for costs incurred and benefits received. These provisions do not apply to contracts where the parties have expressly provided for frustration (e.g., by including a force majeure clause), to contracts for the carriage of goods by sea, to marine insurance or to contracts for the sale of specific goods which perish before risk has passed to the buyer (which is covered by the *Sale of Goods Acts 1979/1994*).

3.4.4   Breach

A breach of contract occurs when:

* a party prior to performance states that he/she will not fulfil his/her obligations, or demonstrates an intention not to fulfil them
* a party fails to fulfil his/her obligations
* a party fulfils his/her obligations in a defective manner.

An indication that a contract will be breached in the future is called repudiation or an anticipatory breach, and may be expressed in words or implied from conduct. The repudiation of a contract entitles the injured party to treat the contract as discharged, and to sue for damages. The same procedure applies if there is an actual breach of a condition, often referred to as a fundamental breach, or breach of an innominate term where the consequences are serious. In the case of both an anticipatory breach and an actual breach, the injured party may choose to affirm the contract. Where actual breach is a breach of warranty or an innominate term where the consequences are insufficiently serious to allow for discharge, the injured party may sue for damages only.

Confusingly, the process of treating a contract as discharged for breach is sometimes also referred to as rescission (see Section 3.1), though it is not usually possible to put the parties back to the positions they were in before the contract began. Although sums due must be paid and incurred obligations honoured, the effect of breach is to end the contract for the future, so that no future obligations arise. The victim must take all possible steps to advise the wrongdoer that he/she regards the contract as discharged, within a reasonable period of time. This may not be possible. For example, the wrongdoer may have fled, in which case it is sufficient to make public the intention to end the contract, inform the police, etc. Where goods are delivered to a buyer and there is a breach of contract, it is enough for the buyer to tell the seller that he rejects them. He need not send them back, though he must not do anything to the goods which may imply that they have been accepted. What constitutes a reasonable time period in this context will depend on a court's view of facts in a particular case.

3.5   Remedies for breach of contract

If a contract or part of a contract is not wholly performed, the other party has various remedies available, namely specific performance, injunction and damages. These are discussed in more detail below.

3.5.1   Specific performance

In some instances, justice will only be done if the wrongdoer is commanded to perform or not perform a specific action. Hence the courts may award an order for specific performance. This orders the wrongdoer to carry out his/her contractual promises(s). If he/she does not do so, he/she will be held in contempt of court, and will suffer the appropriate penalties. An order for specific performance is an equitable, discretionary remedy. (In common law, damages may be claimed as of right.)

A decree of specific performance is rarely granted if damages would be adequate (usually the case if similar goods/services can be obtained readily from another source). If they cannot, then specific performance may be granted, provided that the court is sure that enforcement can be ensured. Contracts of a personal nature, such as employment, which depend on good faith, will not be enforced.

3.5.2 Injunction

An injunction is an order from the court instructing a person not to break a contract. It is also an equitable remedy. It may be used to compel someone to adhere to a promise not to do something, such as enforcing a valid restraint of trade clause to prevent a former employee working for another employer. In *Warner Bros v Nelson* [1937] 1 KB 209,[4] an injunction was issued to forbid the actress, Bette Davis, from working for another film studio.

3.5.3 Damages

As you have already learned, damages are monies paid by the party in breach to place the injured party in the position they would have been in if the contract had been fully performed. Damages may be liquidated damages, which are a sum fixed in advance by the parties as the amount to be paid in the event of a breach. They will be recoverable if the sum fixed was a fair estimate of the likely consequences of a breach, but not if they are in the nature of a penalty. Unliquidated damages are where the court fixes the amount. Nominal damages are awarded if no actual loss is suffered, for instance, where a seller sells elsewhere goods that a buyer has refused. They acknowledge that there has been a breach and vindicate the claimant's rights.

Remoteness and causation

The breach of contract must be the effective cause of the wronged party's loss. However, an injured party cannot recover damages for all potential consequences flowing from the breach, otherwise the liability would be limitless. The loss must not be too remote. What is meant by 'remote' in this context is shown in the case of *Hadley v Baxendale* (1854) 9 Ex 341. In this case there was a delay in repairing the broken crankshaft of a mill, which meant that it stood idle for longer than necessary. Damages were awarded to the mill owner in terms of what was considered to arise fairly and reasonably, and naturally from the breach, and to the extent that loss could be reasonably foreseen by both parties at the time of contracting. In this case the mill owner's claim for loss of profits did not succeed as the repairer did not know that the mill could not be operated at all without the crankshaft. These

---

[4] An English case because the actress (using her married name), although an American, had entered the second contract in England.

principles have been applied to many cases, and this is still the leading case in respect of tests applied to remoteness of loss.

Measure

Most types of loss arising from breach of contract can be recovered – that is, financial loss in terms of expenditure incurred by the claimant in relying on the contract, and, sometimes, loss of profits too, if the claimant suffers lost profits when the contract ends. Loss of future profits may be recovered if it is fairly certain that they would have been made, but not loss of speculative profits. In *Anglia Television v Reed* [1972] 1 QB 60, the defendant broke his contract to act in a television play. The television company recovered their costs in preparing the play, but could not claim any profits they might have made, as these were purely speculative.

Damages may be awarded too for bodily injury, distress or disappointment and loss of valuable reputation.

Mitigation of loss by the claimant

It is the claimant's duty to take all reasonable steps to try to minimise any loss. A seller is expected to try to find another buyer if the originally contracted buyer rejects goods.

Contributory negligence

If a contract imposes a duty of care (such as in dealing with a professional, like a lawyer or an accountant), and this duty is breached, but the claimant has shown contributory negligence, then the claimant's damages may be reduced.

The Limitation Act 1980

Contractual obligations cannot be enforced indefinitely, and after a certain length of time become unenforceable. Although it may still be possible to carry out obligations, there is no legal remedy if a dispute arises. The *Limitation Act 1980* sets out the time periods in which an action must be brought in respect of different issues.

Activity 3.6

In *Koufos v C. Czarnikow Ltd, The Heron II* [1967] 3 WLR 1491, the claimant chartered a ship, The Heron II, to carry a cargo of sugar to Basrah. In breach of the conditions of charter, the ship deviated from an agreed route, which delayed its arrival by nine days. During that period of nine days, the market price of sugar fell. How do you think the court decided on a claim for damages? Which criteria would it apply?

Feedback

The issue is whether a breach of contract is the effective cause of the wronged party's loss, and whether the loss is remote.

In this case, the deviation from an agreed route was a breach of contract which caused delay, and the delay on getting goods to market meant that they could not be sold at the higher market price which prevailed at the time the ship would normally have arrived at Basrah. Asquith, LJ said that it was reasonably foreseeable that this could happen, and the House of Lords held that the claimant could recover as damages the difference between the price at which the sugar was sold, and the price at which it would have been sold if there had been no delay.

Note that the concept of reasonable foreseeability in contract law is much stricter than for negligence in tort. In contract there must be a serious possibility that particular consequences will result, whereas in tort, a slight possibility is sufficient.

Summary

In this session, you have learned what the elements of a valid contract are and the required forms of contract in specific circumstances. To be valid, contracts need offer and acceptance, contractual capacity, consideration, intention to create legal relations, an absence of vitiating factors, and, of course, performance. For most contracts these things are straightforward, but as you have now seen, there are many problems that can arise when all these elements are not incontrovertibly present.

The law of contract is of great importance in business, and now that you have studied these aspects of it, you will appreciate why accountants need to know about it, as contracts and how their financial outcomes are accounted for can have significant effects on an income statement and balance sheet. In the next session we go on to deal with another specific aspect of law – employment law – which also has various financial ramifications.

SESSION **4** Employment law

Introduction

Upon completion of Session 4 you are expected to be able to:

- explain how 'employees' differ from 'self-employed persons', and the essential elements of a contract of employment
- understand the difference between 'unfair' and 'wrongful' dismissal
- demonstrate awareness of the impact on employers and employees of health and safety legislation and the various pieces of anti-discrimination legislation.

In brief, Session 4 helps you learn about different employment law provisions affecting people who are involved in running businesses both as managers and employees, how these are implemented and the effects of breaching law. Employment law is also important in terms of accounting, as accountants will need to know how to deal with the financial consequences of various aspects of it, such as income tax, national insurance, statutory sick pay, etc., in a set of financial reports. Some of this is specialised and beyond the confines of B291, although you have already dealt with one aspect of this, for example, in terms of accounting for wages in Unit 3. Accountants may also themselves be employers, so will be affected too by the wider aspects of employment law discussed here. You should be aware, though, that the topic of employment law is vast, and can be extremely complicated.

4.1 Employees and self-employed persons

The relationship between an employee and employer is a contractual one. One person (the employee) supplies skills and/or labour to another (the employer) in return for payment. This is sometimes referred to as a contract of service. Therefore, all the rules that you have already learned about contract law also apply to this particular type of contract. However, the employment relationship is also heavily regulated by a large number of Acts of Parliament. The *Factory Acts* (first one in 1802, then a later one in 1833) and a series of nineteenth century acts regulating the relationship between 'master' and 'servant' were the first laws regulating labour relations in the UK. The vast majority of employment law before 1960 was based upon contract law. Since then there has been a significant expansion due, primarily, to the development of ideas about equality, worker protection and the UK's membership of the EU. Worker protection rights are usually necessary to counter the considerable inequality of bargaining power between the parties to an employment contract. However, there are great differences worldwide in the level of protection accorded to workers, with economically developed countries in general according a much greater level of protection than less economically developed countries. For example, in developing countries it is not uncommon to find children being employed and for there to be few regulations about number of hours worked or about the safety of working conditions.

Activity 4.1 ....

Visit the home page of the charity War on Want, via the link on the B291 website.

Read about what the charity does in terms of alleviating working conditions in 'sweatshops' and so on, under 'overseas work' and 'campaigns'.

Being an employee is not the only way in which people can work. They may work for themselves as self-employed individuals and thus offer their services to others as independent contractors. This is commonly referred to as a contract for services. Despite this seeming quite straightforward, it is often quite difficult to determine whether a person is an employee or self-employed. People may prefer to be self-employed for a variety of reasons (e.g., there are some tax advantages), but the law does not always agree that they are independently supplying services to a client and it considers that the 'client' might really be their employer. As a result, a series of tests has been developed to help decide someone's status as employed or self-employed. These tests are discussed below.

4.1.1   The control test

This means that an employer controls how, where and when an employee works, a principle established in *Yewens v Noakes* (1880) 6 QBD 530. In *Walker v Crystal Palace Football Club* [1910] 1 KB 87, it was held that a professional footballer was an employee of his club as it controlled his training, discipline and method of pay. However, the control test is not always appropriate when a person is employed because of his/her technical or specialist knowledge, as an employer may not then have sufficient skill or knowledge to control the manner in which such a person works.

4.1.2   The integration test

If someone's work is regarded as integral to a business, and not just an accessory to it, then that person will normally be regarded as an employee. In *Cassidy v Ministry of Health* [1951] 2 KB 343, the employment status of a hospital doctor was in question. As a doctor has specialist skills, which an employer could not be expected to control directly, the test in *Yewens v Noakes* could not be applied. The court held that the doctor was an employee, as his work was integral to the work of the hospital, not an accessory to it. However, this is difficult to apply in many situations as a sole criterion.

4.1.3   The economic reality test (or multiple test)

Under this test, the court will take account of a number of different factors together, in addition to control and integration, to assess whether a person is employed or self-employed. Typically questions will be asked about, for example, who provides any equipment used in the work; who hires any assistants; who bears the financial risk; who is responsible for investment and management; who profits from good management in the performance of the task; whether an individual is paid regularly; whether regular hours are worked; and whether there is mutuality of obligation (i.e., whether the employer has a duty to offer work, and the employee a duty to accept it). Depending on the answer to these questions, a decision will be taken that an individual is employed or self-employed. The existence of some factors (e.g., regular hours and payment and mutuality of obligation) usually suggests employment rather than self-employment, but cases are not always easy to decide, as the weight given to a factor suggesting employment might be overridden by another suggesting self-employment. The cases discussed below (including those in Section 4.1.4) show how difficult it can be to come to a decision.

In *Ready Mixed Concrete (South East) Ltd v Minister of Pensions and National Insurance* [1968] 2 QB 497, the driver of a concrete mixer lorry was previously employed on a contract of service, but was re-engaged on a different basis. He was to purchase his lorry from the company (painted in the company's colours) on hire purchase, be responsible for running and maintaining it, only deliver the company's product, wear company uniform, be subject to general control by the company and be paid according to work done without deduction of income tax or national insurance. If unable to work, he would hire a replacement driver to ensure that the vehicle continued to be available to the company.

The court considered all factors, but considered that, on balance, the terms of the contract were more consistent with a contract for services rather than of service. The court decision was particularly influenced by the fact that the driver, not the company, carried the risk of profit or loss and that the driver could be reasonably viewed as running his own business. This last factor has been of significance in other cases (*Carmichael v National Power plc* [1999] 1 WLR 2042 and *Market Investigations Ltd v Minister of Social Security* [1969] 2 QB 173), and has almost become a fourth, separate test.

4.1.4 Atypical workers

There are considerable problems in determining the status of atypical workers. In *O'Kelly v Trusthouse Forte plc* [1983] 3 All ER 456, a wine waiter worked on a casual basis at the Grosvenor House banqueting hall. He had no other employment, and was offered work on a more regular basis than other casual workers. He was dismissed along with others for trade union activities. He claimed for unfair dismissal (see Section 4.3.2), but the company contended that such a claim was not open to him since he was self-employed. The company's contention was successful, as the court placed great weight on the lack of mutuality of obligation. In *Nethermere (St Neots) v Taverna and Gardiner* [1984] ILRL 240, the defendants sewed trousers at home using company sewing machines. They were paid on a per item ('piecework') basis at the same rate as the factory workers, and although they could refuse work (e.g., if they were going on holiday), they rarely did so. Following a dispute over holiday pay, they sought to claim unfair dismissal, but the company contended that they could not do so as they were not employees. The court disagreed: they were employees because they had built up over time a mutuality of obligation – the company to provide work and the defendants to accept it.

4.1.5   Why the distinction is important

The difference between whether someone is employed or self-employed is important because certain consequences follow as a result of determination of status. These are as follows.

- Employees receive their pay net of income tax and national insurance, which are deducted by the employer and paid over on their behalf to HM Revenue & Customs (HMRC), whereas self-employed persons are taxed in accordance with the trading income provisions, whereby the system of payment is different for income tax. They also pay national insurance at different rates. You will observe that some of the cases we have mentioned have been brought on behalf of a government minister, and this was usually in relation to national insurance issues.

- Employees receive statutory protection in certain areas, for example, unfair dismissal.

- Employees also receive certain state benefits, such as statutory sick pay, which the self-employed do not.

- There are certain implied terms in a contract of employment, for example, a duty of obedience, which are not implied in a contract for services.

- An employer is, as you have seen under contract law, vicariously liable for the acts of employees when done in the course of the employer's business. Someone using an independent contractor is not liable for their acts, as the contractor is not an employee.

- If an employer becomes insolvent, an employee is a preferential creditor, whereas a self-employed person owed money ranks as an ordinary unsecured creditor.

Activity 4.2   ....

Mr Smith is a skilled audio visual technician, and works in the television industry. Because of the nature of his work, many of his assignments are short-term, with some lasting only a day. He would typically undertake some 200 or more assignments in a year. Whilst on an assignment, he does not generally supply his own equipment, and works under the overall control of the television company for which is he is working at any given time.

State, giving your reasons, whether you think Mr Smith is employed or self-employed.

Feedback   ....

Tending to suggest that Mr Smith is employed is the fact that control is exercised by the entities he works for, that he bears little financial risk and has no responsibility for investment and management, and that he has little opportunity to profit from sound management in the performance of his task. Tending to suggest that he is self-employed is the fact that he undertakes so many different jobs, and that there is apparently no mutuality of obligation: the television companies do not appear to be under any obligation to offer him work or he to accept it. Looking at the facts as a whole, Mr Smith would appear to be self-employed, as the nature of what he does, and the weight the final two factors would carry, would tend to override factors which might suggest employment.

4.2 Essential elements of an employment contract

A contract of employment will contain express terms, terms implied by the courts as a result of case law and terms implied by statute. These are discussed below.

4.2.1 Express terms

Where parties agree terms between themselves, as in any other contract, these are express terms, and may be written or oral. However, under the *Employment Rights Act 1996*, an employer must provide an employee with a written statement of certain details of his/her employment within two months of employment commencing. The statement must include the following:

- pay rates and pay interval (weekly, monthly, etc.)
- job title
- hours of work
- place of work
- length of notice
- disciplinary or grievance procedures
- holiday entitlement
- date of employment commencing.

One month's notice in writing must be given of any changes to the above.

The statement itself does not form a contract unless both parties agree and call it a contract. It may be strong prima facie evidence of a contract, but it is not conclusive.

'There, but for the grace of an ironclad contract go I.'

4.2.2 Terms implied by the courts

The courts have implied various terms into the employment contract for both the employer and the employee. These are as follows.

Duties of the employer

- A duty to pay reasonable remuneration (implied if there is no express term in the contract regarding pay).

- A duty to indemnify the employee where the employee has incurred a necessary expense or a legal liability when working for the employer.

- A duty to provide a safe system of work. An employer has a common law duty to take reasonable care for employees' health and safety at work, which will include appropriate selection of staff and supervision, and ensuring that premises, equipment and materials are safe. What is reasonable will depend on circumstances in each case, such as the likelihood of injury, cost of preventing an injury, the personal characteristics of the employee, etc. If the employer has acted reasonably, then he/she will not be liable at common law.

- In addition, an employer has various statutory duties under the *Factories Act 1961*, the *Offices, Shops and Railway Premises Act 1963*, and the *Health and Safety at Work, etc., Act 1974*, which all regulate working conditions.

'I'm concerned gentlemen. Very concerned!'

- A duty to give reasonable notice of termination of employment. This rarely arises as most contracts contain an express term relating to the exact length of notice or stating that the contract is to be for a fixed term.

- A duty of mutual cooperation. The courts tend to interpret this as meaning that an employer must not behave in a manner which will damage the relationship of trust and confidence between employer and employee.

- Provision of work. While there is no common law duty to provide work, such a term may be implied if failure to provide work will deprive an employee of a benefit contemplated by the contract, for example, if insufficient piecework is provided to enable an employee to earn a reasonable living, or if practice is required to maintain an employee's skills. In *William Hill Organisation Ltd v Tucker* [1998] IRLR 313, it was decided that an insistence on garden leave during a period of notice for an employee, who had terminated his contract to go to work for a competitor, was a breach of contract. This was because Mr Tucker needed to practise his skills as a senior dealer in the area of spread betting, being one of only five individuals authorised to do such work.

- Provision of a reference. An employer is not under an obligation to provide a reference, but if he/she does so, it must be truthful, and the employer owes a duty of care to the subject of the reference (*Spring v Guardian Assurance* [1995] 2 AC 296).

> Spread betting is a type of wagering on the outcome of an event, where the pay-off is based on the accuracy of the wager, rather than on a simple 'win or lose' outcome. A spread is a range of outcomes, and the bet is whether the outcome will be above or below the spread.

Duties of the employee

- A duty to obey lawful and reasonable orders.

- An obligation to exercise reasonable care and skill in the performance of the employee's duties, although what is reasonable will depend on the circumstances. Unless an act of negligence is gross (i.e., substantially worse than might be expected of the average reasonable person), it is usually accepted that a single act of negligence will not result in summary dismissal (dismissal without notice – see Section 4.3.1). Some instances of employee negligence may be so serious that criminal charges may also be involved (as in *Lister v Hesley Hall Ltd* [2002] 1 AC 215, where an employee abused children in his care).

An extension of this duty of care is the employer's duty to indemnify the employee for any damages which he/she has to pay as a result of the employer's vicarious liability for the employee's negligence.

'First you'll have to sign this form, releasing me from any liability.'

- A duty to perform work in a reasonable manner. This is sometimes referred to as a duty of mutual cooperation (as mentioned above). The courts will take into account the reasonableness of the order in terms of whether it will frustrate the commercial objective of the employer, as in the case of *Secretary of State for Employment v ASLEF* [1972] 2 QB 455, where the issue was the extent to which a railway workers' 'work to rule' disrupted the service the employees were there to provide. (The term 'work to rule' is used to describe a form of industrial action in which workers scrupulously observe all regulations for the purpose of slowing down work.)

- A duty to provide personal service. An employee may not delegate his/her work to someone else to do without the employer's express or implied permission.

- A duty to give honest and faithful service. An employee cannot use the employer's property as his/her own, or do work in his/her spare time which competes with that of the employer or damages the employer, although he/she may do spare time work. There is also a duty not to disclose trade secrets to a third party or misuse confidential information acquired in the course of employment. In *Robb v Green* [1895] 2 QB 315, Mr Green, while still employed, copied lists of his employer's customers, with a view to starting his own business. This was held to be a breach of contract, as the employee has a duty to work for, and not against, the employer (see also *Hivac v Park Royal Scientific Equipment* [1946] Ch 169).

'Sorry, but I can't tell you how I magically pop out of the hat: My contract has a non-disclosure clause...'

Activity 4.3 ....

Mr Adams is the managing director of a company supplying materials to shipbuilders. He has accepted a sum of money as commission from a customer who has placed a substantial order with Mr Adams's company for materials to build a series of expensive yachts.

Does the commission belong to Mr Adams or to his company?

Feedback ....

Depending on your perspective, it is possible to look at the commission in different ways. To some people it might seem like a bribe or a 'back-hander'. However, legally, the commission belongs to Mr Adams's company, as it has arisen out of a business transaction carried out by Mr Adams's company, of which he is an employee, albeit a senior employee. The commission would amount to what is termed a '**secret profit**', which Mr Adams is under a duty to account for to his company, otherwise he would be guilty of dishonesty.

4.2.3 Terms implied by statute

There are several specific Acts of Parliament, the terms of which are now implied in contracts of employment. These are discussed below.

Employment Rights Act 1996

This gives employees the right not to be unfairly dismissed, to redundancy pay if made redundant and to a minimum period of notice in respect of termination of contract.

Working Time Regulations 1998

These restrict the hours of work to an average of 48 per week, worked out over a 17 week reference period, and give the right to four weeks' paid leave per year and one non-working day per week. Many employers offer standard conditions which are more generous than this.

Employment Act 2002

This allows the parents of children aged six and under to request flexible working arrangements. An employer must consider any such request seriously and can only reject it on sound business reasons. The Act also introduced paternity and adoption leave.

Equal Pay Act 1970

This deals not only with pay, but also things like holiday and sick leave. An equality clause is implied into all employment contracts where workers of different sex do the same job or different jobs of equal value.

National Minimum Wage Act 1998

This imposes minimum levels of pay.

'We'd like to pay you what you're worth, too, Fenstrom.
Unfortunately, we must conform to the minimum wage law.'

4.3   Wrongful and unfair dismissal

4.3.1   Wrongful dismissal

Wrongful dismissal occurs when an employer terminates a contract of employment without giving proper notice or during its fixed term.

Minimum notice periods

If a period of notice is not agreed as an express term in a contract, then the *Employment Rights Act 1996* imposes minimum notice periods. An employee with at least four weeks' continuous employment is obliged to give an employer at least one week's notice that he/she will terminate the contract of employment. An employer must give the following notice.

- One month's to two years' continuous employment – one week's notice.
- Two years' to 12 years' continuous employment – one week's notice per complete year.
- More than 12 years' continuous employment – 12 weeks' notice.

If an employee is dismissed without any notice, this is referred to as summary dismissal and will usually constitute wrongful dismissal unless an employee waives his/her rights, accepts payment in lieu of notice, repudiates the contract or is in fundamental breach of employment duties (see Section 4.2).

Remedies

An individual who believes that he/she has been wrongfully dismissed may bring a common law action for breach of contract for the wrongful dismissal, by suing in the County Court or High Court for damages. Such an action must be brought within six years of the dismissal. Both employees and independent contractors may make such a claim. An employee may instead bring a claim to the employment tribunal, provided that he/she does so within three months of dismissal, and provided that the claim is for £25,000 or less.

4.3.2   Unfair dismissal

This occurs where an employer terminates a contract without justification. The employer may or may not give notice. Sometimes non-renewal of a fixed term contract may constitute unfair dismissal, or it can be what is known as constructive dismissal. This often occurs where an employer is guilty of a significant breach which goes to the root of the employment contract or shows that he/she no longer intends to be bound by an essential contract term. In such a case, an employee may consider himself/herself constructively dismissed. The *Employment Rights Act 1996, s.95* provides protection for employees who find themselves in this situation. An employee may or may not give notice in such circumstances, but must take action swiftly and resign, as if he/she continues to work in such a situation, then he/she will be considered to affirm the contract and will not be able to treat himself/herself as constructively dismissed. He/she will be able to claim wrongful dismissal against the employer. In *Simmonds v Dowty Seals Ltd* [1978] IRLR 211, Mr Simmonds had been employed to work on the night shift. He resigned when his employer tried to compel him to work on the day shift. It was held that he could treat himself as constructively dismissed, as his employer's conduct had been an attempt to change an express term of the contract.

While a constructive dismissal is usually an unfair dismissal, there are circumstances in which it may not be. In *Savoia v Chiltern Herb Farms Ltd* [1981] 1 IRLR 65, Mr Savoia's employer required him to change jobs, as part of a reorganisation, from supervisor of a packing department to production foreman. He refused on the grounds that he would be exposed to conjunctivitis as a result of heat and smoke, although he refused to submit to a medical examination or provide evidence from his own doctor. It was held, among other things, that the employment tribunal, which had dealt with the matter in the first instance, had been correct in finding that Mr Savoia had been constructively, but fairly, dismissed.

Reasons for dismissal

There are many possible reasons for dismissing an employee. Some of these are deemed automatically unfair, while others are deemed fair by law.

Automatically unfair reasons include:

- victimisation of health and safety complainants or whistleblowers
- pregnancy or the exercise of maternity leave rights
- trade union membership or non-membership activities
- assertion of a statutory right
- unfair selection for redundancy.

If the above apply, then it will not matter how long the employee has been employed (see later, under *The unfair dismissal claim procedure*).

Reasons that are considered fair by law include the following, unless the employer behaved unreasonably or unfairly in using any of these reasons:

- defects in an employee's skills or qualifications
- unacceptable conduct by an employee
- retirement (see later)
- redundancy (see later)
- contravention of statute (e.g., where continued employment would break the law)
- another substantial reason (e.g., conviction of a criminal offence committed off duty – see *Singh v London Country Bus Services Ltd* [1976] IRLR 176).

An employer can only rely on a reason for dismissing a person that he/she knew of at the time of dismissal. For example, finding out that someone had stolen money after a dismissal for another reason could not be used retrospectively (*Devis (W.) & Sons Ltd v Atkins* [1977] AC 931).

The unfair dismissal claim procedure

Before going any further, it will be useful to outline briefly the procedure which an employee alleging unfair dismissal must go through. In general, an employee must have been employed continuously for one year (unless the claim is for one of the reasons deemed automatically unfair, as listed above). He/she must serve a formal grievance notice on the employer. If the situation is not resolved, there is an automatic claim to be heard before an employment tribunal within three months of the dismissal. The employee must prove that he/she was dismissed (there is a presumption raised by the circumstances that the dismissal was unfair), and the employer must prove that the reason for the dismissal is one of the reasons outlined above that are deemed fair by law. If the dismissal is found to be unfair, then the employee is entitled to be reinstated, re-engaged or to receive compensation.

On the issue of whether the dismissal was unfair or not, *s.98(4)* of the *Employment Rights Act 1996* requires that the circumstances of the case be examined to see whether the employer acted reasonably, and that a decision be made 'in accordance with equity and the substantial merits of the case'. Case law has considered the issue of reasonableness from the point of view of the severity of the employee's misconduct, and from that of the employer's procedures adopted in coming to the dismissal decision and the manner in which the dismissal itself was handled.

An employment tribunal or court will take into consideration the extent to which an employer has followed the codes of practice (in respect of warnings, enquiry into alleged misconduct, etc.) issued by the Arbitration, Conciliation and Advisory Service (ACAS), which was illustrated in the case of *Polkey v A.E. Dayton Services Ltd* [1988] ICR 142. The House of Lords stated in this case that if an employer has given fair warning and an opportunity to an employee to show that he/she can do the job, then this will be reasonable in the case of alleged lack of ability. Where misconduct is involved, if the employer investigates properly and fairly and allows the employee an opportunity to defend or mitigate his/her conduct, then this will also be considered reasonable. In the case of redundancy, reasonable employer behaviour will constitute consulting employees likely to be affected, choosing a fair basis for redundancy, and taking steps to minimise its effects by offer of other employment in the same organisation. Where 20 or more employees are likely to be made redundant, and there is a recognised trade union, reasonable consultation will include consulting either the trade union or the employees' elected union representatives.

Retirement

Dismissal on the basis of retirement is deemed fair if it takes effect on or after the default retirement age or the employer's normal retirement age, if one exists. The default retirement age varies from country to country, but at the date of writing in the UK, it is 65. There has, however, been much debate about whether the age of 65 should be changed to a greater age or abolished entirely because it is in breach of an individual's right to choose to work if he/she wants.

At the date of writing, the UK government has suggested abolishing its default retirement age.

An employer must give an employee written notice of the date of intended retirement at least six months in advance and tell him/her of any right to request to continue working. If the employer does not give such notice, he/she may be required to pay compensation, and if the notice is given within two weeks prior to the intended retirement date, the dismissal will be deemed automatically unfair. An employee who wishes to continue working must tell the employer this three months before the proposed retirement date, so that it can be properly considered before that date. If it is not properly considered, then, again, this will constitute an automatically unfair dismissal. An employer may refuse such a request, and this will not be unfair provided that the proper procedure has been followed.

If an employee is unfairly dismissed on the grounds of retirement, the remedies are reinstatement to the same job with no loss of seniority, provided that the employee wants this and it is feasible, or re-engagement, where the employee is given a comparable job. If the employer fails to comply with an order to reinstate or re-engage, then compensation will be awarded in accordance with the age and years of service of the employee, based on his/her losses and expenses. This is all set out in statute. If an employer ignores an order, or the dismissal is unfair because of race, sex or disability discrimination, or the reason given for dismissal is an automatically unfair one, then an additional award can be made.

Activity 4.4 ....

Mr Soper's employer decided to make a number of redundancies because of a downturn in business in the location where he was contracted to work. Employees selected for redundancy were offered two options other than redundancy, namely, relocation to the employer's main factory several hundred miles away or an early retirement package. Mr Soper chose the early retirement package, but then submitted a claim for a redundancy package.

State, giving your reasons, whether his claim is likely to succeed.

Feedback ....

Mr Soper's claim would be unlikely to succeed. His decision to accept an early retirement package terminated his employment by choice. No dismissal has taken place, so there can be no claim for redundancy.

Redundancy

An employee may be dismissed as redundant for several reasons. This may be because his/her employer ceases/diminishes (or intends to cease/diminish) the business purpose for which the employee has been employed, or ceases operating (or intends to do so) in the place where he/she is employed. 'Place' here means the place where a person is customarily employed or any place where his/her contract may require him/her to work.

There have been several cases on determining whether or not a person is redundant. In *Vaux and Associated Breweries v Ward (No. 2)* (1970) 5 ITR 62, for example, a 57 year old barmaid was dismissed in favour of a younger, more glamorous barmaid when a pub was modernised (a discotheque was installed). As there was no change to the work being done, it was held that this could not be a dismissal for redundancy.

In terms of the procedure for unfair dismissal for redundancy, an employee must have been employed continuously for two years, and must make a claim to the employment tribunal within six months of dismissal. He/she must prove the dismissal. The presumption is that the employee is redundant, which the employer must attempt to refute. If the employee is found redundant, the basic award is calculated in the same way as for unfair dismissal.

An employee will not receive redundancy pay if he/she refused an offer of other reasonable employment made before the expiry of the old contract, which should begin within four weeks on the same or suitable terms, with a four week trial period being allowed in the new job. Whether the other job offered is reasonable or such an offer is unreasonably refused are matters the employment tribunal will need to address in the event of a dispute. The onus of proof will lie with the employer.

Activity 4.5 ....

Mrs James is a cook and she was dismissed from her job as a maker of specialist pies, because her employer had decided to stop making them as they had become an unprofitable line. She was replaced by a new cook, whose speciality was celebration cakes, which the employer had been developing as an experimental line and had proved successful.

What is the nature of Mrs James's dismissal?

Feedback ....

Provided that all the appropriate procedures had been followed, it would appear that Mrs James was legitimately made redundant. The need for the particular work she was contracted to do has ceased.

4.4 Anti-discrimination legislation

You learned in Section 4.2.3 that there are several specific Acts of Parliament which insert implied terms into contracts of employment. Some of these terms are concerned inherently with discrimination, such as the *Equal Pay Act 1970*. As a particular result of the development of EC law and its impact on English employment law, there is now a considerable amount of employment law in the area of discrimination, which has been particularly affected by EC developments, which restricts the common law freedom that an employer had to offer employment to whomsoever he/she chooses (*Allen v Flood and Taylor* [1898] AC 1). While we do not have the opportunity here to consider any of this in detail, you should be aware that an employer will be in breach of law if he/she discriminates against a person on the basis of:

- sex or marital status
- sexual orientation
- gender reassignment
- race or ethnic orientation

- disability
- age
- religion or belief
- trade union membership
- fixed term or part time work.

The law in this area is dynamic, and may be expected to develop rapidly. Discrimination work of one kind or another forms a large proportion of the work of employment tribunals.

Summary

In this session you have learned about the difference between employees and self-employed persons, and why this distinction is important. You have also learned about the essential elements of a contract of employment and about wrongful and unfair dismissal and the remedies available. You have also become aware of other legislation designed to protect employees in various ways, such as various health and safety legislation and anti-discriminatory legislation. This session has been a brief introduction to these topics to provide a contextual background for the general operation of business. Now that we have considered various aspects, you should find it easier to understand how particular aspects of employment law may have accounting implications, for example, such as the need to make a provision for future redundancy costs, or the outcome of an action brought by an employee for wrongful or unfair dismissal.

We shall now move on in the next session to look at the law of agency.

SESSION **5 The law of agency**

Introduction

Upon completion of Session 5 you are expected to be able to:

* define what is meant by the terms 'agent' and 'principal'
* explain how an agency relationship is established and understand the concept of authority
* discuss the possible liabilities of both agent and principal.

The terms 'agent' and 'principal' have been mentioned several times in this module, especially in Unit 1, Section 1.2.1, in relation to the concept of stewardship and accountability. The agency relationship also underlies auditing, as discussed in Unit 6. Agency is a very important concept in the work of the accountant and auditor, so here we will consider briefly the law of agency.

5.1 Definition of terminology

An agent is a person authorised to act on behalf of another party, who is referred to as a principal. Sometimes an agency relationship (i.e., a relationship in which an agent is engaged by a principal) is quite explicit, and is something with which we may be familiar in day to day life, for example, employing an estate agent to find a buyer for a house. However, an agency relationship also exists between a director and his/her company, a partner and his/her partnership, and between an accountant or tax consultant when acting on behalf of a client with HMRC.

5.2 Establishment of an agency relationship

The concept of authority is central to the relationship of a principal and agent, as it defines what the agent is empowered to do on behalf of the principal, and the acts for which the principal is liable. There are five ways in which an agency relationship can arise, as follows.

1 By express agreement, where the principal actually appoints an agent, orally or in writing. This means that the agent will be expressly authorised to act. Note that an agency agreement may be embodied in a formal contract, but it need not technically amount to a contract (*Freeman & Lockyer v Buckhurst Properties (Mangal) Ltd* [1964] 2 QB 480).

2 By implied agreement, where there is no express agreement, but the relationship may be implied, for example, from conduct. Implied authority may also arise where an action is incidental to the performance of an authorised act, where it would be normal for an agent in a given position, or where an action has not been expressly forbidden by the principal (*Hely-Hutchinson v Brayhead Ltd* [1968] 1 QB 549).

3 By necessity, where someone may find that he/she has to act in an emergency on behalf of someone he/she cannot get in touch with, for example, storing property that cannot be delivered according to plan (*Great Northern Railway Co v Swaffield* (1873–74) LR 9 Ex 132).

4   By ratification, where an agent exceeds authority or has no authority to act until/unless the principal ratifies the contract after the event (*Kelner v Baxter* (1866–67) LR 2 CP 174).

5   By estoppel, where a principal represents that someone is acting as his/her agent, although that person is not so acting. Such a representation may arise because the supposed agent occupies an office/position where such acts would be normal or because previous dealings by someone as an agent allow an inference of agency to be made for future dealings. In such instances, the agent's authority is said to be apparent or ostensible. However, the principal is then estopped (prevented) from refuting any claim made by that person to have an agent's authority. (See *Summers v Solomon* (1857) 7 El & Bl 879.)

A third party cannot rely on ostensible authority if he/she is aware of a lack of actual authority.

Many of the cases involving company promoters are concerned with their authority or otherwise to act, as they are acting as agents on behalf of persons who wish to form a company (see Sections 6.2.1 and 6.2.2).

Activity 5.1

Samuel advertised a horse, Binky, for sale, which was left at the stables where it was usually looked after on a day to day basis. Meanwhile, Samuel went away on holiday. Joshua saw the advertisement, went to look at the horse and made an offer for it. Nathan, who owned the stables where Binky was kept, accepted the offer on Samuel's behalf.

Advise Samuel as to whether he is bound by the contract.

Feedback

On the facts given, we do not know if Nathan had express authority to act as Samuel's agent. If he did, then Samuel is bound by the contract. Depending on what Nathan actually normally does (e.g., is he a horse trainer who regularly buys and sells horses for owners who stable their horses at his premises?), his authority to act may be implied, or if he had actually acted as an agent for Samuel selling horses in the past, then the authority to act might be ostensible. In either case, Samuel would be bound. If, however, Nathan has no authority to act in the sale of Binky, then Samuel would not be bound unless he chose to ratify the contract within a reasonable time of hearing about it, for example, on his return from holiday. Also, we do not know anything about Joshua. If he is unknown to both Samuel and Nathan, he would be unlikely to know anything about whether Nathan would be authorised to act, but if he knew either Samuel or Nathan or both, he might have knowledge about Nathan's authority to act, and could not rely on it if he knew it to be ostensible.

5.3 Liability

Generally, a contract arising in an agency situation is between the principal and the third party. Usually the existence (but not always the identity) of a principal is known to the third party. In such circumstances, the principal is said to be disclosed. The agent usually has no rights under any contract, nor any liability, except in the following circumstances:

* where the agent indicates an intention to take personal liability, such as by signing his/her own name to a contract

- where liability is usual for a particular trade or by custom
- where the agent refuses, if asked, to identify the principal
- where the principal is fictitious.

Sometimes, however, a third party does not know that a principal is involved, and in such a case, a principal is said to be undisclosed. If the third party discovers the existence of a principal, then he/she may choose to treat either the agent or the principal as bound by the contract.

5.3.1   Agent's duties and rights

The relationship between an agent and principal is a fiduciary one, that is, one of trust. This means that an agent must always act in the principal's best interests. The most important duties are that an agent should not, without express or implied authority, delegate his/her office; he/she should not place himself/herself in a position where agency duties conflict with his/her personal interests; he/she should not accept bribes; he/she should not take advantage of his/her position for personal gain or to make a secret profit; and he/she must account to the principal for all monies held for use or received.

If an agent breaches this fiduciary duty, the principal can repudiate the agency agreement, dismiss the agent without notice, refuse to pay any money owed to the agent, recover any sums already paid and recover any secret profit if one has been made.

Obviously an agent has a right to expect to be paid for work undertaken for a principal, and usually the amount of commission/remuneration will be specified in the agency agreement. If not, a court will imply a term requiring a reasonable sum to be paid. An agent also has a right to claim an indemnity against a principal for expenses reasonably disbursed in carrying out the agent's duties. He/she also has a right to exercise a lien over the principal's property. This means that the agent has a right to retain any of the principal's property which is lawfully in his/her possession until any debts due to the agent from the principal have been settled.

5.3.2   Termination of the agency agreement

There are two main ways in which an agency agreement may be terminated – by the conscious act/decision of the parties or by operation of law – which are discussed below.

By conscious act/decision of the parties

An agency will normally end when an agent has carried out the task agreed, or by the passing of time if the agent was employed to act for a specific period of time. If there has been a formal agency agreement, the parties can also agree to a voluntary discharge of their agreement, and in the case of ordinary agency agreements, either party can usually end the agreement by giving notice of an intention to withdraw. If, however, the agreement derives from a formal contract, a principal may be liable for damages if the agent's contract is prematurely terminated. Special rules apply if the agreement is with a commercial agent. The law also distinguishes between irrevocable agency agreements (where the underlying purpose is to secure or protect an agent's interest; where the agent has carried out some part of his/her duties; or where statute in certain instances protects parties against the effects of a revocation of authority) and revocable ones (where the principal is free to revoke the agent's authority, provided that his/her obligations have not already been fulfilled).

By operation of law

An agency agreement can be terminated by operation of law, independently of the will of the agent or principal, in four main ways: by death of one of the parties (unless the agency is deemed an irrevocable one); by insanity of one of the parties; by bankruptcy of either party; and by frustration, where the agency agreement derives from a formal contract and an event renders the contract illegal, impossible, etc.

Summary

Session 5 has briefly examined the law of agency, and you should now know what is meant by the terms 'agent' and 'principal', the importance of authority, how an agency relationship is established and what the possible liabilities are of both agent and principal. You will also understand how important the concept of agency is in the work of an accountant and auditor. We shall now move on in the next session to look at the law in reference to different types of business entity, especially companies.

SESSION 6 Legal matters associated with company form and formation

Introduction

Upon completion of Session 6 you are expected to be able to:

* understand the implications of corporate personality, such as the 'veil of incorporation' and when this may be lifted, and the corporate capacity to contract

* demonstrate awareness of the procedure for registering a company, the advantages of purchasing a company 'off the shelf', and the purpose, legal status and contents of the Memorandum and Articles of Association and other company documents, such as statutory books.

Sessions 6 and 7 consider certain aspects of company law. Most countries have specific laws governing companies (sometimes referred to as corporations). In the UK, the primary legislation is the *Companies Act 2006*, which has already been mentioned a number of times in this unit. UK company law has developed over many years, and there have been many different Acts of Parliament dealing with it. The *Companies Act 2006* is one of the longest pieces of legislation ever enacted by the UK Parliament, and has made changes to almost every aspect of law in respect of companies. It codifies a number of common law principles, such as those relating to directors' duties, and is explicit in its references to international accounting standards in terms of the format of financial statements, etc. Consequently, it is legislation of great significance for accountants. However, we cannot cover all its many facets in this unit, so we concentrate on developing in more detail topics that have already been introduced in B291.

Session 6 develops from a legal perspective some of the concepts and topics that you have already learned about in Units 1 and 5. You learned in Unit 1 about the essential legal characteristics of, and differences between, various types of business entity, such as sole traders, partnerships and various forms of company (e.g., public and private, limited by shares, limited by guarantee, etc.). In Unit 5 you learned about the different types of regulations which govern preparation of their financial statements, and the advantages and disadvantages of carrying on business using a particular legal form. Session 6 looks further at the legalities associated with companies, in terms of their legal personality, their capacity to make contracts, and legal issues associated with setting them up. This type of legal knowledge forms part of the professional 'tool kit' of accountants as they may act as a company auditor or as a professional adviser, and sometimes as a company secretary.

6.1 The implications of corporate personality

6.1.1 The veil of incorporation

As you learned in Unit 1, a company is a legal person. This means that it has a legal personality separate from the individuals/entities who/which own its shares. This was enshrined in a well known case,

Salomon v Salomon & Co Ltd [1897] AC 2. In this case, Mr Salomon transferred his business to a limited company (i.e., he incorporated it). He was the majority shareholder and a secured creditor. The company went into liquidation, and the other creditors tried to obtain repayment from Mr Salomon personally. It was held by the House of Lords that Mr Salomon as a shareholder and director had no liability to these other creditors, and as a secured creditor himself, he could be repaid in priority to the other creditors. Although Mr Salomon owned the majority of the shares, the creditors were not allowed to look behind the company itself to try to obtain their money from the shareholders. This has held true ever since and this concept is referred to as the veil of incorporation or sometimes as the corporate veil. In *Macaura v Northern Life Assurance* [1925] AC 619, Mr Macaura sold a forest to a company in which he owned all the shares. However, he continued an insurance policy on the forest in his own name, not that of the company. When the forest was destroyed by fire, Mr Macaura could not claim on the insurance policy as the company owned the forest, and despite being a shareholder in the company, he did not own the property.

6.1.2 Other results of incorporation

In addition to the veil of incorporation, separate legal personality has other consequences, as outlined below.

- A company can make contracts in its own name and so can sue and be sued. It is also liable in tort for any injuries sustained as a consequence of its agents' or employees' actions.

- Similarly, if injury is done to a company, the company itself, acting through the majority of its members, must take remedial action, as decided in the 1843 case of *Foss v Harbottle* 67 ER 189. A corollary of this is that an individual cannot raise a legal action in response to a wrong suffered by the company.

- As *Salomon v Salomon* shows, a company is responsible for its own debts. If it becomes insolvent, the shareholders are not liable for its debts. However, if shareholders have not paid up any capital (on shares or on guarantees) which they have agreed to contribute, then they can be asked to pay up such amounts at any time. Likewise, a company's directors are separated from its owners, unless the directors also happen to own shares.

- A company can own property in its own name.

- Although it is a legal person, a company does not cease to exist if its shareholders die. It has what is termed 'perpetual succession', and the shares are passed to other individuals. However, a company's existence can be ended through a formal winding up procedure.

- Companies are subject to the rules set out in the *Companies Act 2006*.

Activity 6.1   ....

In the case of *Wilson v Jones* (1867) LR 2 Exch 139, Mr Jones was a shareholder in the Atlantic Telegraph Company and took out a marine insurance policy on the business venture to lay a telegraph cable from Ireland to Newfoundland. This was unsuccessful. Did he have a right to claim on the insurance policy?

Feedback   ....

The case depended on what exactly was being insured here (again, apply the principles of analysis you learned in Activity 1.1). From the later case of *Macaura v Northern Life Assurance*, we know that Mr Jones would not be able to claim if he had insured any property that belonged to the company, as he was a shareholder and would have no insurable claim. However, the court held that Mr Jones had not insured company property, but had insured the profits that he had himself expected to derive from the business venture, which he lost – and he was allowed to recover them, via a claim to the insurance company.

6.1.3   Lifting the veil of incorporation

In certain circumstances, it is permitted to look behind the veil of incorporation. This is often referred to as 'lifting/piercing the veil of incorporation'. Usually where this is allowed, it will mean that the shareholders or directors will become personally liable for the company's debts. Lifting the veil of incorporation has often been permitted (though by no means always) where there has been little separation between ownership of companies and control.

The occasions when the veil may be lifted are determined by statute and by case law.

By statute

If a public limited company begins to trade without having first obtained a **trading certificate** (see Section 6.3.2), the directors under *s.767* of *Companies Act 2006* may be made liable personally for any loss sustained by a third party.

If a director who is disqualified from acting as a director under the *Company Directors (Disqualification) Act 1986* nonetheless acts as a director, he/she will be jointly or severally liable for the company's debts.

If directors and/or members undertake wrongful or fraudulent trading, then they may be personally liable under the *Insolvency Act 1986* for resultant losses arising.

By case law

Sham companies

Per *Woolfson v Strathclyde Regional Council* 1978 SC (HL) 90, the veil of incorporation may be lifted if special circumstances exist which suggest that it is a facade and conceals the true facts, in other words, if it is a sham. For example, in *Gilford Motor Co Ltd v Horne* [1933] Ch 935, Mr Horne set up a company in competition to Gilford. Mr Horne himself had a personal contract with Gilford restraining him from acting in competition with that company. The court held that Mr Horne had set up his own company as a way of evading his own legal obligations, so it was prepared to lift the veil of incorporation and also to restrain Mr Horne's company from competing with Gilford.

Times of war

In times of war, when it is illegal to trade with an enemy, the court has been prepared to lift the veil of incorporation. In the case of *Daimler Co Ltd v Continental Tyre & Rubber Co (Great Britain) Ltd* [1916] 2 AC 307, the defendant was a company incorporated in the UK, but was owned by a company incorporated in Germany and a number of other shareholders, all of whom were German, apart from one who was British, and who owned one share. The claimants owed a debt to the defendants, but the court held that they need not pay it, as the defendant company was effectively owned by the enemy and to pay the debt would constitute trading with an enemy. Thus the court lifted the veil of incorporation to identify the nationality of its members.

Groups

Although any company is a separate legal entity, there have been instances where the court has been prepared to lift the veil of incorporation in a group of companies, that is, between a holding company and a subsidiary. In *DHN Food Distributors v London Borough of Tower Hamlets* [1976] 1 WLR 852, it was done to give the group a higher compensation payment on the compulsory purchase of premises. DHN's subsidiary, which had no business activities, owned the said premises, but DHN used them for its own business purposes. Both companies had the same set of directors. The local authority refused to pay the compensation to DHN because it did not own the premises. The court decided that the two companies in this case should be regarded as a single economic entity, so DHN should receive compensation. However, more recent cases (*Adams v Cape Industries plc* [1990] Ch 433) have cast doubt on this decision, and suggest that the courts would be more reluctant to ignore separate legal personality. In *Adams v Cape Industries plc*, the Court of Appeal refused to lift the veil between Cape and one of its subsidiaries to enable a court judgment against the subsidiary to be enforced against Cape.

6.2 Pre-formation activities

6.2.1 Promoters

The case of *Twycross v Grant* 2 CPD 469 established that a company promoter is a person (excluding anyone acting in a professional capacity, such as a solicitor) who undertakes to form a company and take the necessary steps to do so under a promotion contract.

A promoter has a fiduciary duty to disclose any interest in transactions to the company and not to make a secret profit, and likewise to disclose any benefit acquired to an independent board and/or the shareholders. If he/she does make such a secret profit, the company may rescind the promotion contract. However, this may not be feasible if a third party has acquired rights under the contract. The company may obtain damages if it can prove that it has sustained a loss. The company may also recover the secret profit if it can be proved that the promoter did not disclose it to the company.

6.2.2 Pre-incorporation contracts

This is a contract made by a person on behalf of a company before it is legally formed. This person is often a company promoter, as the company does not have contractual capacity until it is incorporated. In such a case, the person making the contract is personally liable. This was the case at common law, and is confirmed by several cases (e.g., the 1866 case of *Kelner v Baxter* LR 2 CP 174), and now by *s.51* of the *Companies Act 2006*. To refute liability, per *Phonogram Ltd v Lane* [1982] QB 938, clear and express words are required.

However, a promoter may do certain things to protect himself/herself from legal action, such as waiting to finalise the contract until after the company has been incorporated or agreeing that there will be no personal liability. He/she can also include in the contract a term which gives the company the right to sue under the *Contracts (Rights of Third Parties) Act 1999*. He/she may also enter a contract of novation. This involves ending (discharging) the original contract and creating a new one or transferring the contract to someone else (assigning it). Another means of protection is to use an off the shelf company, which is discussed in Section 6.2.3.

6.2.3 Off the shelf companies

An off the shelf company is one already formed. A promoter may buy one of these. It means that the company can trade and make contracts immediately and so prevents the problems associated with pre-incorporation contracts. It is usually also quite a cheap and simple solution, but a potential disadvantage is that the Articles of Association (see Section 6.3.4) may not be appropriate. Formal procedures exist whereby they can be changed, but this involves a degree of expense and inconvenience.

6.3 Forming a company

Setting up/forming a company, which is also referred to as incorporating, requires a number of formal procedures. These are discussed below.

6.3.1 Registration

In the UK today, most companies are incorporated by the process of registration with the Registrar of Companies at Companies House. This means that certain documents must be submitted to the Registrar to form the company. The complete list is as follows.

- Memorandum of Association. This is a document signed by all subscribers stating that they wish to form a company and agreeing to become members of the company (they will be the initial shareholders).

- Application form. This must include the proposed company name, whether the members will have limited liability (by shares or guarantee), whether the company will be public or private, and where its registered office will be. This application form must also include details of the first director(s) of the company.

- Articles of Association. If no articles are provided, the model articles will apply (see Section 6.3.4).
- Statement of capital and initial shareholdings. This must provide details of the number of shares, their aggregate nominal value and how much has been paid up.
- Statement of guarantee. This applies only to companies limited by guarantee, and states the maximum amount each member agrees to contribute.
- Statement of proposed officers. This gives the names and details of the first directors, and company secretary, if applicable, and their consent to act.
- Statement of compliance. This confirms that the registration procedure, etc., has been carried out in accordance with the *Companies Act 2006*.
- Registration fee.

When the Registrar has received the documents listed above, he/she must inspect them to ensure that they meet the *Companies Act 2006* requirements, and issue a certificate of incorporation as proof that they have been met. The company's formal existence starts from the date of the certificate of incorporation.

6.3.2   Trading certificate – public companies

Public limited companies (though not private limited companies) must have a trading certificate, issued by the Registrar, before they may trade. To obtain such a certificate, a formal application to the Registrar must be made, which states:

- that the nominal value of the allotted share capital is equal to or greater than £250,000
- that at least a quarter of the nominal value and all of the share premium have been paid up
- the amount of preliminary expenses and who has paid or will pay them
- any benefits given or to be given to company promoters (see Section 6.2.1).

If a public company trades before it has a trading certificate, then there are grounds to wind up the company if it is not obtained within one year. The company and any of its officers who are in default may be fined. It will be a criminal offence for the company to trade, although any contracts made will be binding on the company. However, the directors will be personally liable if the company defaults within 21 days of the due date for contract completion.

6.3.3   Company name

There are several rules with which a company must comply in its choice of name. As we have already seen in Unit 1, if the company is a public limited one, it must have 'plc' (with slight variations being possible) at the end of its name, and if it is a private company, it must have 'limited' or 'ltd' (permitted variations are detailed in Unit 1, Session 2). In addition, it:

- Cannot have the same name as another company in the index of company names.
- Cannot use certain words which are deemed offensive or are illegal.
- Must have the permission of the Secretary of State to use certain words (e.g., 'England', 'Chartered', 'Royal', 'National', 'University', 'Insurance') and any others which suggest a connection with the government or any local authority.
- Must avoid the tort of **passing off**. Passing off is conducting business so as to mislead the public into thinking that one's goods or services are those of another business. This most typically occurs when goods are marketed with a design, packaging or trade name that is very similar to that of someone else's goods, but the concept can apply to a company name (or the name of any other legal form of business) as well. In the case of *Harrods Ltd v R. Harrod Ltd* (1923) 41 RPC 74, the famous Knightsbridge store was successful in preventing a money-lending company from trading under the Harrods name. Although there was a difference in business, it was felt that that the public might assume that they were connected.

The Secretary of State has the power to make a company change its name if it is the same as another company's or too like it; if the name gives a misleading indication of the company's activities, such that it may harm the public; and if misleading details were provided when applying to use a name that required approval.

6.3.4 Articles of Association

This document sets out the company's internal constitution, namely how the company and how the relationship between the company and its shareholders will be governed. A company may draft its own articles as the contents of the articles are not governed by law. If a company is formed without registering articles, the model articles set out in the *Companies Act 2006* will apply. If its registered articles do not expressly exclude or modify the model articles, then, again, the model articles will apply. A company may also choose to adopt the model articles in whole or in part, if it wishes.

Alteration of articles

It is possible to alter the Articles of Association after they have been adopted. This usually requires a **special resolution** (see Table 3) and a 75 per cent majority of shareholders voting in favour. Copies of the amended articles must be sent to the Registrar within 15 days of the resolution being passed. If articles are deemed to be **entrenched**, then a specified procedure (e.g., unanimous consent) may be required to change them.

A shareholder cannot be bound by any alteration passed after he/she became a member that requires an increase in liability or contribution to the company.

In common law, a change to the articles must be deemed to be bona fide (i.e., made in good faith) and in the interest of the company as a whole (*Allen v Gold Reefs of West Africa Ltd* [1900] 1 Ch 656). The onus is on the members to decide whether a change is bona fide and in the interest of the company as a whole (*Greenhalgh v Arderne Cinemas Ltd* [1951] Ch 286), and the court will not intervene unless a reasonable person would not consider the change bona fide (*Brown v British Abrasive Wheel Co* [1919] 1 Ch 290). If a change is bona fide, it is irrelevant if it causes hardship or operates retrospectively. A change will be void, however, if actual fraud or oppression takes place. A change will not be invalid simply because it causes a breach of contract, although the injured party can sue for the breach. In *Southern Foundries (1926) Ltd and Federated Foundries Ltd v Shirlaw* [1940] AC 701, alteration of the articles gave the company the power to remove the managing director, but he then had the right to sue for breach of contract.

Company resolutions

Resolutions are how companies take decisions, and will be referred to frequently in subsequent sections. There are three basic kinds, as Table 3 makes clear.

Table 3 Different kinds of resolutions

Type	% of votes required to pass	Purpose	Does the Registrar need to be advised?
Special	≥ 75%	Many purposes, including altering the company name, winding up the company, altering the Articles of Association, altering share capital, approving various sorts of transactions with directors, or if the Articles of Association require it for specific types of transactions.	Yes, within 15 days.
Ordinary	> 50%	Used when statute requires, or if the Articles of Association do not require a special resolution.	Only if the law requires.
Written (private companies only)	As for a general meeting.	May be used for anything which does not require special notice (28 days). Members cannot change their written vote and the date a written resolution is passed is when the required majority is reached. It must be passed within 28 days from its circulation.	Yes, if a 75% majority is required.

Legal effect of the Articles of Association

A company's Articles of Association form an enforceable contract between the company and its members, and between the members themselves, even though the members do not sign the articles. This is now enshrined in *s.33* of the *Companies Act 2006*, but a number of prior cases had established this (e.g., *Hickman v Kent or Romney Sheepbreeders' Association* [1915] 1 Ch 881; *Pender v Lushington* (1877) 6 ChD 70; and *Rayfield v Hands* [1958] 2 WLR 851). The articles do not bind the company to non-members (*Eley v Positive Government Security Life Assurance Co Ltd* (1876) 1 ExD 88; *Beattie v E. & F. Beattie Ltd* [1938] Ch 708; *New British Iron Co, Re, ex parte Beckwith* [1898] 1 Ch 324). In the *Eley* case, the articles provided that Eley, a company member, should be solicitor to the company and when the company decided to employ other solicitors, he sued for damages. He failed because, although he was a member, he was attempting to enforce his contract as a solicitor, not as a company member.

6.4 Statutory books, returns and records

6.4.1 Statutory books

A company must by law maintain a number of formal records which are referred to as statutory books. A list follows of the individual records which must be maintained.

- Register of members. This contains the names, addresses, the dates someone became a member and/or ceased to be so, the number and class of shares held, and the amount paid up.

- Register of directors. This contains the names of directors, their address, occupation, nationality, other directorships which they have held within the previous five years and date of birth. (Service addresses (e.g., the company's registered office) and personal addresses must be recorded, and, although the company will need to supply both to the Registrar of Companies via its annual return (see Section 6.4.2), it will withhold personal addresses from the publicly available register.)

'I'm a company director too, but I'm not letting my home address go on public record.'

- **Register of company secretaries.** This contains similar information to the register of directors.
- **Register of directors' interest in shares and debentures.**
- **Directors' service contracts.**
- **Register of charges.** This contains a list of certain charges, with the name of the chargee, details of the type of charge, the property charged, the amount of the charge and the date created.
- **Minute books** of general meetings and directors' meetings.
- Accounting records.

The statutory books are normally kept and maintained at the company's registered office (although the register of members and register of directors' interests may be kept where they are written). All records may be inspected free of charge by members (except for the directors' minute book and the accounting records), must be made available for public inspection for up to two hours a day and may not be closed to public inspection for more than 30 days in any year.

You have already learned in Units 5 and 6 about the type of accounting records that must be maintained and the type of financial statements which must be produced.

6.4.2 Annual return

A company must file an annual return with the Register of Companies each year, within 28 days of the return date, which is the anniversary of the company's incorporation. The annual return contains the following details:

- the address of the registered office
- the type of company
- the company's principal business activities
- required particulars of the company's directors and company secretary/ies
- issued shares and who holds them
- whether the company was a traded company at any time during the return period
- a statement of capital
- where company records are kept if other than at the company's registered office (and the records that are kept at that other location)
- **private company elections** in place to dispense with holding annual general meetings or filing financial statements.

Activity 6.2 ....

Donald Drake and Michael Mouse have just qualified as accountants and want to set up in business as a partnership to provide a standard range of accountancy services to the local area in which they live. They are thinking of using the trading name of 'Donald's and Micky's accountancy services' (feeling that this is informal and friendly), and of having a logo which shows a duck and a mouse. However, a friend points out to them that they might be in danger of committing the tort of passing off, because their trading name, combined with use of the logo, could imply a likeness with certain cartoon characters which are well known worldwide. Is the friend right?

Feedback   ....

In general, a business organisation may choose whatever name it likes. It must not, however, be the same as or too close to that of any other business, nor must it be so misleading as to harm the public (or the Secretary of State could order it to be changed).

On the facts here, Donald and Michael could be committing the tort of passing off, although the difference in types of business (accountancy services and cartoon film entertainment) might militate against the idea. Would anyone really think that a cartoon film entertainment company would be offering accountancy services? However, the use of the logo with a duck and a mouse suggests that Donald and Micky might be thinking of using another organisation's name and goodwill to their own advantage, though much might depend on how similar the logo is to the cartoon characters. On balance, it might be better if Donald and Micky did not use this particular logo, although they would be unlikely to find any problem with the use of the name of 'Donald's and Micky's accountancy services', as they are using their own names here.

Summary

In Session 6 you have learned more about aspects of corporate personality, such as the 'veil of incorporation' and when this may be lifted, and the corporate capacity to contract. You have also learned about the procedure for registering a company, pre-formation activities, the advantages of purchasing a company 'off the shelf', and the purpose, legal status and contents of the Memorandum and Articles of Association and other formation documents. You have also become aware of the purpose of statutory books. In the next session, you will learn more about company administration and finance, much of which is dictated by the type of legal form. As with Session 6, this all forms part of the legal knowledge 'tool kit' for accountants.

SESSION **7 Company administration and finance**

Introduction

Upon completion of Session 7 you are expected to be able to:

- explain the purpose of meetings of a company's board of directors and the procedures involved, voting rights, etc.

- explain the reasons and procedures for the appointment, retirement, disqualification and removal of directors, and understand their duties and powers while in office

- explain the qualifications, powers and duties of the company secretary

- understand the different types of shares a company may issue, the procedures for issuing them, acceptable forms of payment and differences in rights which may be attached to different types of shares

- explain the purpose of shareholders' meetings (annual and extraordinary), when they are used and the procedures which are involved, including the different types of shareholder resolutions

- identify, compare and contrast directors' and shareholders' rights and powers and understand the different rights held by majority and minority shareholders

- understand the ability of a company to take on secured and unsecured loans and the nature and effect of fixed and floating charges and relevant procedures

- demonstrate awareness of the concept of capital maintenance for a company and the reasons for which share capital may be issued, redeemed, reduced or repurchased.

Session 7 considers the basic concepts and principles underlying company administration, with reference to directors, shareholders and the company secretary, and finance, in terms of share and loan capital. Again, this type of legal knowledge forms part of the accountant's 'tool kit' and is needed especially in his/her role of employee, auditor or professional adviser.

7.1 Directors

7.1.1 The power conferred upon directors

In theory, decisions about how a company should be run fall upon its members, and although members retain certain rights (see below), they usually delegate the day to day responsibility of company management to a board of directors. Directors are required to run the company in accordance with the constitution of the company as set out in the objects clause of the Memorandum of Association. Until relatively recently, the objects were often defined narrowly, which restricted what directors were empowered to do and could result in them and the company acting *ultra vires* (beyond their legal power). However, under *Companies Act 2006*, objects are not restricted unless the Articles of Association specifically restrict them.

While individual directors may be responsible for specific company functions (e.g., finance, sales, etc.), it is the job of the board of directors as a whole, not individual directors, to manage the company. This management will be effected by a series of regular meetings, often monthly, where decisions will be taken on matters put before the board to be discussed and voted on in terms of action to be taken. If passed (usually requiring a majority of board members, though specific rules can be set out in the Articles of Association), measures are implemented, and then reported back on to the board at subsequent meetings. Minutes of these meetings will be kept, and form one of the company's statutory documents (see Section 6.4.1). If the company's articles delegate to the board responsibility for running the company, the members cannot interfere in their decisions, as directors are not subject to their instruction on how to act (*John Shaw and Sons (Salford), Ltd v Peter Shaw and John Shaw* [1935] 2 KB 113). However, despite this, members do retain power where a special resolution is required for action to be taken. They can also, if they see fit, pass an ordinary resolution to remove a director if their views are ignored; and they can, by special resolution, amend the Articles of Association, which could include a restriction on directors' powers.

7.1.2 Types of directors

The word 'director' means, per *s.250* of the *Companies Act 2006*, 'any person occupying the position of director, by whatever name called'. This means that a director may actually be called something other than a director, as the definition is based on the function carried out. Companies, as legal persons, can act as directors of other companies, but at least one company director must be what is termed a 'natural person' (meaning a human being), who must be aged 16 or more. There are several different kinds of directors, as discussed below.

- **Managing director (MD)**. The MD is a member of the board and usually an executive officer, taking a lead role in management of the company. The model articles allow the board to delegate to the MD any powers they deem appropriate. Sometimes the MD is referred to as the **Chief Executive Officer (CEO)**.

- **Executive director**. This is a member of the board active in company management and likely to be a full time employee.

- **Non-executive director (NED)**. An NED is not usually an employee of the company, but someone from outside the company who brings in expertise of a particular kind on a part time basis. In general, NEDs act as a check on the activities of the executive directors.

- **Chairperson (of the board)**. This is a director who chairs the meetings of the board of directors and quite frequently acts as a spokesperson for the company, for example, in giving media interviews. The Chairperson should generally be someone other than the CEO. Refer back to Unit 6, Activity 2.3, on the issue of Stuart Rose acting both as CEO and Chairman for Marks & Spencer in contravention of the *Combined Code on Corporate Governance* (2008) (now *The UK Corporate Governance Code* (2010)).

An individual director cannot take a decision which binds the company without being given express authority to do so. Authority may, however, in certain circumstances be implied or ostensible and will be binding. For example, the MD has implied authority to bind the company in the same way as the board. Ostensible authority is where a particular director is considered by other directors as having the power to bind the company.

Even if directors' authority to act is limited, it will still bind the company as long as the other party acts in good faith. Actual knowledge by the other party of a limitation in authority does not generally constitute a lack of good faith. However, if a third party to a transaction is a director or a person associated with him/her (e.g., wife, husband, certain other relatives, business partner, etc.), then the company can void the transaction and is entitled to obtain compensation from the parties involved.

7.1.3 Appointment, disqualification and removal of directors

Appointment

Directors are usually appointed by the current directors or by a members' ordinary resolution (although the first directors will be named in the Articles of Association without such a procedure). If the company is a public one, then *s.160* of the *Companies Act 2006* requires that they be voted on individually by company members. If a director is appointed improperly, then, despite this, per *s.161* of the *Companies Act 2006*, his/her actions remain valid.

Public companies require a minimum of two directors, whereas private companies require only one. There is no statutory cap on the number of directors a company may have, although the Articles of Association may decree a maximum number.

At the first annual general meeting (AGM) (see Section 7.4.1), all the directors retire and may offer themselves for re-election if proposed by a members' ordinary resolution. A director's service contract cannot exceed two years (*Companies Act 2006, s.188*) unless this has been approved by the shareholders by ordinary resolution. As you may remember from Section 6.4.1, a register of directors' service contracts must be kept at the registered office and made available for public inspection. Any casual vacancies arising on the board (e.g., because someone dies or unexpectedly leaves office) may be filled by the board, but such new officers must stand for election at the next AGM.

One third of the NEDs, usually the most senior, must also retire at each AGM. They can, however, be re-elected. The company must notify Companies House within 14 days of any new director appointments and also of any changes in details (e.g., change of residential address), and must record details in the register of directors (see Section 6.4.1).

If a director receives compensation for loss of office, and this is gratuitous on behalf of the company, then it must be disclosed to members and approved by ordinary resolution. If the members do not approve, then the director will hold the payment on constructive trust for the company.

Disqualification

Per the model articles, a director must vacate his/her office if he/she does not attend board meetings for a period of six months or if he/she becomes insane or bankrupt, as these events disqualify a director from acting. The *Company Directors (Disqualification) Act 1986* provides additional reasons for disqualification. These are as follows.

(a) Misuse of company limited liability status, where directors might set up a new company to carry on the same business as an old one which had unpaid debts.

(b) Conviction of a serious offence in relation to the management of a company (such as persistent default in filing annual returns).

(c) Fraudulent or wrongful trading.

(d) Unfitness to manage a company following an investigation by the Department for Business, Innovation and Skills or as stated in a liquidator's report.

In the case of (a) to (d) above, the maximum period of disqualification is 15 years, with a two year minimum in the case of a liquidator's finding.

If a disqualified director continues to act when disqualified, this is actually a criminal offence and can carry both a fine and a term of imprisonment as penalties. He/she will also be personally liable for any company debts incurred when he/she so acted, as will any person acting knowingly on a disqualified director's instructions.

Removal

Under *s.168* of the *Companies Act 2006*, the members of a company can, by ordinary resolution, remove a director from office before his/her period of office comes to an end, despite any provision in its Articles of Association, any agreement made with him/her or any provision in the director's service contract. If such a removal breaches a director's contract, he/she can sue for damages.

Special notice of 28 days of this ordinary resolution is required, to be provided to the director in question and to all members eligible to attend the meeting to vote on the resolution, with a copy of the resolution going to the director. The director has the right to ask the company to circulate his/her written representations to members and can read them out at the meeting if there was insufficient time before the meeting to circulate them. He/she must be allowed to attend the meeting and to speak. In *Bushell v Faith* [1970] AC 1099, a provision in the Articles of Association to give a threefold weighting to shares owned by directors, if there was any attempt to remove a director, was held valid as the law only requires an ordinary resolution and is silent on how this might be obtained or defeated.

7.1.4 Duties of directors

The *Companies Act 2006* sets out specifically the general duties of directors. Hitherto these had been a mixed bag of common law rules and equity as demonstrated by various decisions in case law. While case law has been superseded by statute, the cases are still germane to the application of the new law. The general duties of directors are discussed below.

- Directors have a duty to act in accordance with the Articles of Association and use directorial powers solely for the purpose given, otherwise a transaction will be void (although shareholders can ratify it after the event if they choose, as was evidenced in *Hogg v Cramphorn* [1967] Ch 254).

- They also have a duty to act in good faith which promotes the commercial well-being of the company and the entirety of its members. This means that they must consider the long-term outcome of decisions, employees' interests, relationships with customers, suppliers, etc., the company's impact on the community, its reputation and so on.

- Directors have a duty to act independently, subject to agreements made by the company to which it must adhere and to the Articles of Association.

- They must act with care, skill and diligence (see Session 5, on the law of agency). The standard to be applied here is what might be reasonably expected of a director generally and of a particular director's knowledge, skill and experience. If, for example, a director is an accountant, he/she would be expected to use those accountancy skills to the benefit of the company (as was set out in *Dorchester Finance Co Ltd v Stebbing* [1989] BCLC 498).

- There is also an obligation incumbent upon directors to avoid situations where there is a conflict of interest between them and the company or in performance of other duties.

- There are rules too to prevent directors from profiting from their position. They must not accept any benefits from any third parties which arise simply as a result of a person being a director. Similarly, if a director has an interest in any transaction or arrangement that the company proposes, he/she must make this known, in writing, at a board meeting or by a general notice. Activities which violate these duties would be a breach of a director's fiduciary duties.

Consequences of a breach of directors' duties

Directors' duties are owed to the shareholders as a collective body (i.e., the entire company), not as individuals. If a director is in breach of a duty, then he/she may have to make good any loss the company suffers as a result. A company can also recover any of its property the director or a third party might have unless the third party obtained it bona fide. A breach can be prevented by an injunction.

A company may choose to ratify a breach of duty by ordinary resolution, but any attempt to exempt a director from liability for a breach of duty/negligence is void.

Activity 7.1

The facts of the case of *Percival v Wright* [1902] 2 Ch 421 are basically as follows. Certain shareholders offered to sell shares to directors who knew that the true value of the shares was greater because of an impending take-over bid, which their duty of confidence to the company forbade them to disclose. The shareholders tried to have the contract of sale rescinded. Could they succeed?

Feedback

The shareholders could not rescind the contract, as the duty of the directors required keeping confidential the negotiations in respect of the take-over bid which would affect the price. They had no duty of disclosure to these shareholders, but would have to the company as a whole. Given what you have learned about ethics in Unit 6, you may feel that the directors would have faced a considerable ethical dilemma here, but this case still reflects the law as it currently stands.

7.2 Company secretary

A company secretary is another type of company officer. There is only usually one company secretary at a given time. While every public company must have one, private companies may choose to do so, but are not required by law to have one. A plc company secretary must possess formal qualifications in that he/she must be one of the following: barrister, solicitor, member of one of the four English accounting institutes or of the Institute of Chartered Secretaries and Administrators (ICSA). Being qualified to do the job by reason of another position or qualification also constitutes an adequate qualification, as does having been a plc company secretary for three out of the last five years. (Note that the law is unclear as to how one might become a company secretary by this last route if one did not have appropriate qualifications in the first place.)

The job of a company secretary is not defined by law and the board of directors may set out specifically what it should be. Usually, the company secretary has responsibility for issues concerning formal company documentation, in that he/she maintains the statutory books, submits returns to the Registrar of Companies, deals with formal shareholders' meetings and their administration, keeps minutes of meetings, etc.

The company secretary has the authority to make contracts to bind the company if given authority by the board, but has ostensible authority in relation to administrative contracts, such as hiring cars, etc. (*Panorama Developments (Guildford) Ltd v Fidelis Furnishing Fabrics Ltd* [1971] 2 QB 711).

7.3 Shares and shareholders

In this section, we consider in more detail the administrative aspects of owning shares.

7.3.1 Different types of shares and rights attached

You have already learned in Unit 1 and Unit 5 about the different types of shares that a company can issue as one means of raising finance. These are basically ordinary shares and preference shares, which may be redeemable or irredeemable and cumulative or non-cumulative.

Unit 5 also introduced the idea of authorised share capital, which is the total nominal value of the shares that a registered company is authorised to issue (details of which must be set out in the Articles of Association). For example, a company may have an authorised share capital of £20,000, divided into 20,000 shares of £1 nominal value. If it issues 15,000 of these shares, it is said to have an issued capital of £15,000. Its unissued capital will be £5,000, and it may issue up to 5,000 £1 shares in the future. If the company has received the full nominal value of the shares issued, then this amount of capital is said to be fully paid up. However, a company may not require shareholders to pay in full for shares issued, but may ask them to pay, say, half of the nominal value. In such a case the shares issued would be 50 per cent paid up. It may then ask in due course for a further 25 per cent of the nominal value. This is referred to as a call for payment, and would leave 25 per cent therefore uncalled. Note that a call for payment should be distinguished from an instalment, which is just a means of payment allowing a call to be paid over time.

A company can alter (reduce, increase or reorganise) its authorised share capital if its Articles of Association permit. If they do not, alteration can still be done by ordinary resolution.

You also encountered the terms bonus share/issue and rights issue in Unit 5. A bonus share is a share issued to existing shareholders in proportion to their shareholding, for example, one bonus share for every four shares held, sometimes expressed as a ratio (e.g., 1:4). A shareholder does not pay for a bonus share, but the company must account for the issue by a debit (for the nominal value) to reserves (usually retained earnings, although a company may set up a capital redemption reserve or use a share premium account, if it has one, to deal with these sorts of transactions) and a credit to the share capital account. Bonus issues are often used in a reorganisation of a company's share capital structure. In a rights issue, new shares are offered to existing shareholders in proportion to their existing shareholding in the same way as for bonus shares, but they must pay for them, as the purpose of a rights issue is to raise new finance. The shares are usually offered at a price less than the current market value, but not less than nominal value, as this would be illegal. Existing shareholders are not obliged to take up the rights issue. If they do not, the shares can be sold to others and existing shareholders will receive the proceeds.

A company may also issue different classes of shares, which we have seen in terms of preference shares being a different class from ordinary shares. However, a company can also issue different sub-classes of both preference and ordinary shares, which may have a different nominal value and carry different rights. For example, a company may issue ordinary 'A' shares and ordinary 'B' shares. Different classes of shares have different rights attached to them which concern voting, dividends and distribution of capital on winding up.

Ordinary shares carry full voting rights in respect of all matters on which ordinary shareholders are entitled to vote, subject to sub-class variations. Preference shares carry no rights or restricted rights. Preference shareholders have a fixed dividend (usually expressed as a percentage of the nominal value and payable every six months). This is paid before ordinary dividends, which are not fixed. Preference shareholders are entitled to a return of their capital in a winding up in priority to ordinary shareholders, but do not have the latter's right to a share of any surplus assets after all debts and dues have been paid.

Class rights can be varied, however. If a procedure to vary rights is set out in the Articles of Association, then this must be followed. If it is not, then, per *s.630* of the *Companies Act 2006*, variation requires a special resolution or the written consent of 75 per cent of the nominal value of the shares in the class to be varied. However, the holders of 15 per cent (or more) of the nominal value of that class, who did not consent to the variation, may petition the court to cancel the variation within 21 days of the passing of the motion to do so. The court may confirm the variation in question, or may cancel it if the petitioner can prove that it is unfairly prejudicial.

7.3.2 Rights at company meetings

Shareholders have the right to attend company meetings and vote at them, in accordance with the rights granted by the class of share held.

7.3.3 Issuing shares and payment for shares

A company's Articles of Association may empower directors to issue shares (the usual term is 'allot' shares), but if not, they need to be given specific authority to do so by the members passing an ordinary resolution. The authority given must be clear as to the number of shares which can be allotted and the date when the authority expires (it can only last for a maximum of five years).

Shares may be issued at a premium on the nominal value. As you will remember, this must be credited to a share premium account. The share premium account may only be used to write off the expenses relating to this issue of shares and any commission paid, and to issue bonus shares, as you learned earlier in this session.

In terms of paying for shares, any sort of shares (other than bonus shares, for obvious reasons) may be paid for in cash, whether issued by a private or a public company. For a public company, the subscribers to the Memorandum must actually pay in cash for their subscription shares. Payment by non-cash consideration is also permitted, but for a public company's shares this must not be in the form of work or services, must be received within five years of issue and must be independently valued and reported on by a person who is qualified to act as the company's auditor. In the case of a private company, no such formal process is required to value non-cash consideration, though it can be challenged in court if it appears inappropriate. It should also be noted that a public company cannot allot shares until a quarter of their nominal value and all the share premium (if any) have been paid up.

7.4 Company meetings

7.4.1 Types of meetings

Owning shares gives shareholders the right to attend company meetings and vote in accordance with the rights that their particular class of share grants. Meetings must be quorate (i.e., they need generally two members or their proxies) to be deemed competent to transact business. Members usually vote by a show of hands (one member equals one vote, regardless of the number of shares held) unless a poll (counting the number of shares voting for or against a resolution) is requested, which would override any show of hands. A poll may be requested by members who own 10 per cent at least of the voting rights in total or by no fewer than five members permitted to vote on the resolution in question.

There are three types of company meeting, the annual general meeting (AGM), general meetings (GM) and class meetings, which are discussed below.

Annual general meeting

This is held once a year, and although private companies are not legally obliged to hold one, many do. The business of the AGM is to consider the company's financial statements, appoint an auditor (if the company is required to appoint one), elect directors and declare dividends. Public companies must hold their AGM within six months of their financial year end, and if it is not held, the company and its officers can be fined. A period of 21 days' notice (which must state that the meeting is an AGM) is required unless all entitled to attend and vote agree to a shorter period. Members have a right to propose a resolution for the AGM agenda and to require the company to circulate details of it to all members. (If the resolution is proposed after the financial year end, the members proposing it must cover the cost of circulation.) Such a resolution requires the support of members holding five per cent or more of the voting rights or 100 members or more holding an average £100 of paid up capital.

General meetings

This kind of meeting may be held whenever it is needed, and must be held by a plc if its net assets have fallen to less than half of its called up share capital. A general meeting is any meeting that is not an annual general meeting, and, before the advent of *Companies Act 2006*, used to be referred to as an extraordinary general meeting (EGM). Notice of 14 days is required unless shareholders with at least 95 per cent of the shares agree to a shorter period. If the company is private, this can be reduced to 90 per cent.

Class meetings

This is a meeting of a particular class of shareholders, typically held to consider a variation of the rights of their class. It requires 14 days' notice and to be quorate, that is, two persons must be present who hold at least one third of the nominal value of the issued shares of the particular class.

7.4.2   Power to call a meeting

The directors, members, an auditor who is resigning and the court all have the power in certain circumstances to convene a company meeting. The Articles of Association usually give authority to directors to call a meeting, but the members can also require the directors to do so. Members holding ten per cent or more of the paid up voting capital (if a private company, five per cent if more than 12 months have passed since the last GM) can require directors to call a GM, and the directors must call it within 21 days of this request. The meeting must then take place within 21 days of the notice being given. The members themselves who made the request (or any members holding in excess of 50 per cent of the total voting rights) may call a meeting themselves within three months of the original request if the directors do not do so, and may recover their expenses from the company.

A resigning auditor has the right to ask the directors to call a meeting so that he/she can explain the reasons for his resignation in person, and the court can call a meeting at the request of a member or director if other means of doing so are not feasible.

7.4.3   Notice

Notice is an important concept in terms of meetings and has been mentioned above. Every director and member is entitled to receive notice of all meetings (including date, time, place, nature of business and the text of any special resolutions), although accidental failure to notify anyone entitled to notice does not render the meeting invalid. The number of days' notice varies, depending on the type of meeting, with 21 days in general being required for an AGM and 14 for a GM, subject to the reductions discussed above for AGMs and GMs if members agree. Some resolutions (e.g., for the removal of an auditor or a director) require special notice of 28 days.

7.4.4 Minority rights

Given that most resolutions require a majority of 75 per cent or over 50 per cent of the votes cast to be passed, there can still be a substantial body of shareholders who are not in favour of a resolution. These are referred to as minority shareholders and if they are unhappy with a decision, they have various remedies open to them, depending on a combination of their level of voting rights and the issue to which they object. For example, they can defeat a special resolution to alter the company's name/articles, reduce share capital or wind up the company, if they have 25 per cent or more of the voting rights. The situation in respect of minority shareholders can be complex legally, as shareholders can exercise their votes as they wish, and if this is done in good faith for the benefit of the company as a whole, the grounds for an action by a minority are hard to argue. (Could not any majority decision be argued as discriminating against the minority?) However, the court can take action to regulate a company's affairs for the future and restrain the (continued) performance of prejudicial acts.

Activity 7.2

Mr Harmer senior formed a stamp auctioning company which was joined by two of his sons, as directors, when they left school. Mr Harmer was chairman of the company and the articles gave him a casting vote. Together with his wife, who always voted with her husband, he controlled all aspects of the company. The sons claimed that their father had repeatedly abused his controlling power in the conduct of the company's affairs. He was an autocrat who took all decisions himself and believed that no director should hold a contrary view to his own. He made a number of unprofitable decisions, despite the protests of his sons, drew down unauthorised expenses for his wife and himself and engaged a private detective to watch the staff. Would the sons' claims succeed?

Feedback

The above are the facts of *Re H R Harmer Ltd* [1959] 1 WLR 62. The court granted relief which included an order that Mr Harmer senior should henceforth be employed as a consultant by the company on a specified salary and that he should not interfere with the affairs of the company. The order went on to provide that he be appointed president of the company for life, but that this office should not impose any duties or create any powers for him in relation to the company.

7.5 Loan finance

7.5.1 Debentures

Companies may raise funds by issuing shares, as you have learned, but they may also borrow money in various ways to raise funds. All companies have an implied power to borrow money to carry on their business. They can borrow money from banks (usually, but not always, merchant banks), but can also issue various types of formal debt instruments, as you will remember from Unit 1, Section 3.3.1. These debt instruments are referred to by different names, such as bonds, debentures or loan stock, all of which can be used inexactly as terms of description. However, debentures and loan stock in terms of companies are interchangeable terms, and we shall here consider them and refer to them as debentures.

A bond is an instrument issued by borrowers which has a par/nominal value (e.g., £100), a promised interest rate which can be fixed (e.g., 8 per cent), or floating (e.g., 2 per cent above **LIBOR**), and a maturity date (e.g., 2020). Bonds are typically issued by public companies, governments or local authorities and some are traded by investors in the stock markets. The rules relating to the issue of publicly tradable bonds are complex and beyond the scope of this module.

A debenture is evidenced by a formal document issued by the company which acknowledges its indebtedness, and will generally set out the terms of the loan, for example, rates of interest, dates the interest is payable (usually every six months), repayment of capital, etc. It is common for a debenture to be secured or charged on a company's assets, but it need not be. Being secured on an asset means that if the company defaults on interest/capital repayments, the lender has the right to have the asset sold to recoup monies owed.

There are both advantages and disadvantages to issuing debentures as compared with shares. They are usually cheaper to issue and may be issued at a discount. There are fewer restrictions on redemption, and they do not 'dilute' control of the company as they do not carry voting rights. The board does not usually need to be authorised by a general meeting to issue them, and the interest payable is an allowable deduction from profits for corporate tax purposes. However, companies in financial difficulty may find it difficult to pay the required interest, so failure to pay may compel lenders to instigate liquidation and/or administration procedures, if the debentures are secured. Also, if companies have a high level of debentures (and/or other loans) in comparison with share capital, they are said to have high gearing, and this adversely affects the market price of public company shares.

7.5.2 Security for debentures

You learned above that it is common for a debenture to be secured/charged on a company's asset(s). There are two types of charges – fixed charges and floating charges, which are discussed below.

Fixed charges

A fixed charge is a legal/equitable mortgage on a specific, identified asset (often land and/or buildings). The effect is that the company cannot do anything to or with the asset without the chargee's agreement, for example, sell it, as the asset is intended to be kept by the company, until at least the period of charge comes to an end.

Floating charges

A floating charge, described by Slade, J:

> remains unattached to any particular property and leaves the company with a licence to deal with, and even sell, the assets falling within its ambit in the ordinary course of the business.
>
> *Re Bond Worth Ltd* [1980] Ch 228, at 266

Romer, LJ in *Re Yorkshire Woolcombers Ltd* [1903] 2 Ch 284, at 295, also described a floating charge similarly, but indicated that it could attach to a particular class of assets which would typically change from time to time. It has been, therefore, a useful device for obtaining security over a company's current assets which frequently change during a normal trading cycle, as it allows a company to deal freely with such assets, and provides a wider range of assets that can be charged. However, there is no reason that a floating charge cannot also 'hover' (the word used by Lord Macnaghten in *Illingworth v Houldsworth* [1904] AC 355, at 358) over land and buildings, though as specific assets, which typically change infrequently, these are more usually the subject of a fixed charge or mortgage.

However, a floating charge does not attach to any particular asset until crystallisation occurs. This means that, for example, an event specified in the debenture document occurs, such as the company being unable to pay its debts, especially the debenture interest. The company ceasing to trade or going into liquidation will also cause a floating charge to crystallise. Crystallisation also reveals the disadvantages of a floating charge, in that the value of the security may be uncertain until then. A floating charge also has lower priority than any fixed charge and a liquidator may be able to ignore it if it was created within 12 months of any winding up.

Priority and registration of charges

The priority of a charge for repayment depends on the type of charge and whether or not it has been registered with the Registrar of Companies, which must be done within 21 days of creation of the charge by either the company or the chargee. If the charge is not registered, if created within 12 months of winding up, a liquidator may ignore it. Non-registration also results in the company and all officers in default being fined and makes the money borrowed repayable at once.

A company must also include the charge in its own register of charges, although failure to do so does not render the charge invalid.

A fixed charge has priority over a floating charge, but if charges are equal, then the first created has priority. A registered charge has priority over an unregistered registerable one. A chargeholder may prevent the creation of a later charge with priority provided that any later chargee has notice of both the prohibition and the charge.

7.6 Capital maintenance

Now that we have considered the ways in which a company may raise capital, we turn to the subject of maintaining that capital. The idea behind capital maintenance is that a company should not be able to reduce its capital (by returning it to members), as the capital acts as a 'buffer fund' in accounting terms so that creditors are not disadvantaged in the event of a winding up. In this context we are dealing only with share capital: loan capital is not subject to capital maintenance.

7.6.1   Reduction of capital

In spite of what has been stated above, there are occasions on which a company can reduce its capital at any time (*Companies Act 2006, s.641*). For example, it may do the following.

(a) Reduce or cancel liabilities on partly paid shares, thus foregoing any claim for monies owing.

(b) Return capital in excess of the company's needs, by repaying cash to shareholders.

(c) Cancel paid up share capital that is no longer represented by assets. For example, if a company has accumulated losses, rather than profits, it can write this off by reducing share capital. This may be done in different ways, depending on whether shareholders and/or other stakeholders bear the losses, and is often done as part of a capital reconstruction scheme.

(d) Purchase its own shares (considered separately in Section 7.6.2).

There are specific procedures which must be followed. A special resolution must be passed and the court applied to for confirmation of the special resolution. In the case of (a) and (b) above, the court must require companies to pay creditors who are entitled to object to these kinds of proceedings and will not confirm the reduction until satisfied that all creditors have been paid or agree to the reduction. If the company is a plc, it must file documents with the Registrar of Companies if the share capital falls below £50,000.

There is a simplified form of the above procedure if the company is a private one. A private company must still pass a special resolution, but this must be supported by a solvency statement from the directors, stating that the company will be able to pay its debts in the forthcoming year. If such a statement is made unreasonably, then it is an offence punishable by a fine and/or imprisonment. Copies of the resolution, the solvency statement and a statement of capital must be filed with the Registrar of Companies within 15 days.

7.6.2   Purchase of own shares

In certain circumstances, a company may purchase its own shares. This might take the form of redeeming redeemable preference shares, where this was always envisaged. In terms of ordinary shares, reasons may be different, such as to try to prevent a hostile takeover bid, or to create shareholder value by reducing the number of shares in issue to increase earnings per share and/or by reducing dividend distribution costs.

For a share repurchase to happen, the company's Articles of Association must allow it; the shares which are to be purchased must be fully paid; the purchased shares must be cancelled; and the company must formally advise the Registrar of Companies of all this, within one month (accompanied by a revised statement of capital).

In terms of finance for the repurchase, companies may use the proceeds of a new issue, or may transfer from distributable profits an amount (equal to the par value of the shares to be purchased) to a capital redemption reserve. Companies may make a purchase on the stock exchange or purchase directly from a shareholder.

Private companies additionally can purchase shares out of capital, but there are specified procedures for this. A statutory declaration is required from directors that the company can pay its debts as they fall due in the next year, which must be supported by a report from the auditors. The declaration and the report must be made available to members prior to the passing of the resolution approving the payment, otherwise it will be invalid. Within a week of the directors' declaration, a special resolution must be passed, and a public notice put in the *London Gazette* within one week of the resolution so that any creditors desirous of preventing the payment can apply to the court to do so. Payment out of capital must occur within five to seven weeks after the resolution and all documents must be filed with the Registrar of Companies.

Share repurchases must, of course, be accounted for in the company's books and records. However, this is beyond the scope of this module, and you are not expected to be able to account for share repurchases.

The *London Gazette* is one of the official newspapers of the British government, in which certain statutory or official notices are required to be published.

7.7 Distributions

Companies can only pay dividends out of profits that are deemed distributable. In general, directors recommend the payment of a dividend and the company declares it by passing an ordinary resolution in the AGM. 'Distributable' means accumulated realised profits less accumulated realised losses (in so far as not utilised already). It therefore excludes any revaluation reserve, and for a public company, also excludes any share premium account, any capital redemption reserve, any other unrealised profits, and any reserves the company is not allowed to distribute. In calculating the amount of distributable profits, the *Companies Act 2006* stipulates that 'relevant accounts' must be used. These are compiled using either UK GAAP or EU adopted IFRS, and will usually be audited accounts. (Note that under IFRSs, some unrealised gains and losses flow directly to the income statement (profit and loss account), but these are not distributable.)

Summary

In Session 7 you have learned about the basic concepts and principles underlying company administration (with reference to directors, shareholders and the company secretary), and finance (in terms of share and loan capital, especially debentures). An accountant needs to know how to account in company records and financial statements for finance raised or repaid, interest payable and due, and dividends, so this kind of legal knowledge is an important part of the legal 'tool kit' for an accountant working in a company or for one acting as an auditor or professional adviser.

Unit summary

In Unit 7, you have learned more about the legal environment in which business operates. You have looked generally at the different types of law and legal systems to provide a context for examining more closely specific areas relevant to business, such as the law of tort, the law of contract, employment law and the law of agency. From there you have proceeded to consider legal issues concerning company form and formation and have moved on to examine company administration and finance. It has been emphasised throughout how important it is for an accountant to know about these topics as they affect the work of an accountant in various ways, either when working for a company, as a member of an accounting firm acting as an auditor, or as a professional adviser.

The following self-assessed questions provide you with the opportunity to check whether you have understood the material in this unit.

Self-assessed
Questions

Please note that in the suggested answers that follow each of these questions, the answers are only given briefly in outline form, with a cross reference to the section(s) of the main text where relevant material is provided. Full written answers are not provided, as writing styles, how people include content and discuss it, etc., can be different from individual to individual, and answers which may look very different can each be good, original, and even creative. There are several ways, for example, of writing an effective answer to any question, but you should always avoid being descriptive or giving 'lists', and aim to provide critical or analytical discussion. The answer style, too, will depend on the type of question. These self-assessed questions are representative of the type of essay questions that could be set in the unseen examination at the end of the module. However, in law, it is quite possible to have questions that require legal analysis of a particular scenario or scenarios, as in many of the activities you have already worked on, so you should be prepared for this type of question as well. The approach to be adopted in the case of scenarios should follow that used in the feedback to Activity 1.1. Remember too that written answers need a proper introduction and conclusion, should be as full as the time allowed permits (a maximum of 45 minutes for an unseen examination question) and should be written in good English with proper use of grammar, syntax and punctuation.

Question 1

Why do financial accountants need to be familiar with aspects of business law?

Suggested answer

The introduction and summary section to each of the main sessions (in this unit) contain suggestions that will be useful in addressing this question. The underlying idea is that businesses operate in an environment governed by a variety of laws (tort, contract, agency, employment, and specific company law) which will have particular effects or outcomes. Very many of these effects or outcomes will be financial, hence an accountant, either one working for a company or acting for a company client (as auditor, professional adviser) will need to know how to account for them in a set of company records and financial statements.

Question 2

By reference to decided cases, explain how the concept of negligence has developed in the twentieth and early twenty-first centuries, and what its relevance is to the work of an accountant.

Suggested answer

The material to answer this question is contained in Session 2, especially Sections 2.2 and 2.5.

Question 3

Discuss how, in contract law, the concepts of practical (or subjective) consideration and promissory estoppel may be used as different legal ways to develop a solution to a legal problem.

Suggested answer

The material to answer this question is contained in Section 3.2.4.

Question 4

Compare and contrast the rights and duties of shareholders and directors of a limited company.

Suggested answer

The material to answer this question is contained in Sections 7.1.1, 7.1.4, 7.3 and 7.4.

Further reading

Please make sure that you consult the latest edition of any textbook you might choose to read (whether one of those below or others). Some textbooks are published annually, so please check carefully that you are not reading out of date material.

Bell, A.C., *Employment Law,* London, Thomson/Sweet & Maxwell.

Elliott, C. & Quinn, F., *Tort Law*, UK, Pearson/Longman.

French, D., Mayson, S. & Ryan, C., *Company Law,* Oxford, OUP.

McKendrick, E., *Contract Law – Text, Cases and Materials*, Oxford, OUP.

Munday, R.J.C., *Agency: Law and Principles*, Oxford, OUP.

Slapper, G. & Kelly, D., *The English Legal System*, UK, Routledge.

Module summary

As this is the end of Unit 7, you have now come to the end of B291 *Financial accounting*. Congratulations on reaching this point in your studies. This module commenced with a general introduction to many topics, which the different units then covered in greater depth. You have now studied a considerable amount of material, which has taken you through understanding the purpose and context of financial accounting and reporting, learning double-entry bookkeeping, and preparing different kinds of financial statements (for sole traders, partnerships and companies). This is summarised in the flowchart below, which you will remember from Unit 2.

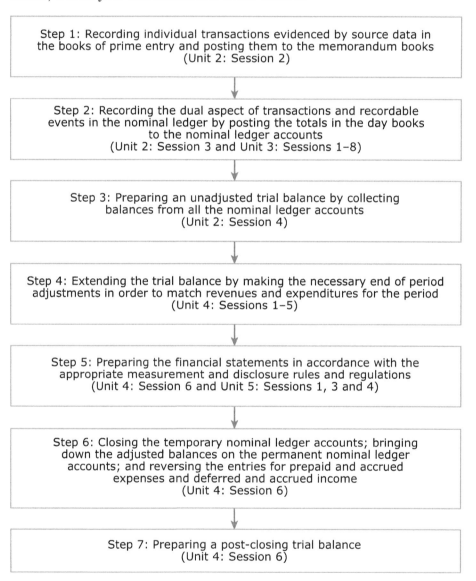

Step 1: Recording individual transactions evidenced by source data in the books of prime entry and posting them to the memorandum books
(Unit 2: Session 2)

Step 2: Recording the dual aspect of transactions and recordable events in the nominal ledger by posting the totals in the day books to the nominal ledger accounts
(Unit 2: Session 3 and Unit 3: Sessions 1–8)

Step 3: Preparing an unadjusted trial balance by collecting balances from all the nominal ledger accounts
(Unit 2: Session 4)

Step 4: Extending the trial balance by making the necessary end of period adjustments in order to match revenues and expenditures for the period
(Unit 4: Sessions 1–5)

Step 5: Preparing the financial statements in accordance with the appropriate measurement and disclosure rules and regulations
(Unit 4: Session 6 and Unit 5: Sessions 1, 3 and 4)

Step 6: Closing the temporary nominal ledger accounts; bringing down the adjusted balances on the permanent nominal ledger accounts; and reversing the entries for prepaid and accrued expenses and deferred and accrued income
(Unit 4: Session 6)

Step 7: Preparing a post-closing trial balance
(Unit 4: Session 6)

Figure 3   The accounting cycle

In addition, you have learned in Units 6 and 7 about ethics, corporate governance, corporate social responsibility, auditing and law and their relevance to financial accounting and the various forms of work undertaken by an accountant. The knowledge and practice that you have acquired from undertaking this module will provide you with a sound basis to go on to study B292 *Management accounting*, and then on to further professional accounting examinations if you so choose. We wish you well in your future studies.

References

Table of statutes

Convention for the Protection of Human Rights and Fundamental Freedoms, ETS 5 (European Convention on Human Rights, Rome, 1950).

Great Britain. *Animals Act 1971. Elizabeth II. Chapter 22.* (1971) London: The Stationery Office.

Great Britain. *Companies Act 2006. Elizabeth II. Chapter 46.* (2006) London: The Stationery Office.

Great Britain. *Company Directors (Disqualification) Act 1986. Elizabeth II. Chapter 46.* (1986) London: The Stationery Office.

Great Britain. *Consumer Credit Act 1974. Elizabeth II. Chapter 39.* (1974) London: The Stationery Office.

Great Britain. *Consumer Credit Act 2006. Elizabeth II. Chapter 14.* (2006) London: The Stationery Office.

Great Britain. *Consumer Protection Act 1987. Elizabeth II. Chapter 43.* (1987) London: The Stationery Office.

Great Britain. *Contracts (Rights of Third Parties) Act 1999. Elizabeth II. Chapter 31.* (1999) London: The Stationery Office.

Great Britain. *Dangerous Dogs Act 1991. Elizabeth II. Chapter 65.* (1991) London: The Stationery Office.

Great Britain. *Employment Rights Act 1996. Elizabeth II. Chapter 18.* (1996) London: The Stationery Office.

Great Britain. *Employment Act 2002. Elizabeth II. Chapter 22.* (2002) London: The Stationery Office.

Great Britain. *Equal Pay Act 1970. Elizabeth II. Chapter 41.* (1970) London: The Stationery Office.

Great Britain. *Factories Act 1961. Elizabeth II. Chapter 34.* (1961) London: The Stationery Office.

Great Britain. *Fair Trading Act 1973. Elizabeth II. Chapter 41.* (1973) London: The Stationery Office.

Great Britain. *Health and Safety at Work, etc., Act 1974. Elizabeth II. Chapter 37.* (1974) London: The Stationery Office.

Great Britain. *Human Rights Act 1998. Elizabeth II. Chapter 42.* (1998) London: The Stationery Office.

Great Britain. *Insolvency Act 1986. Elizabeth II. Chapter 39.* (1986) London: The Stationery Office.

Great Britain. *Law Reform (Frustrated Contracts) Act 1943. Elizabeth II. Chapter 40.* (1943) London: The Stationery Office.

Great Britain. *Law of Property (Miscellaneous Provisions) Act 1989. Elizabeth II. Chapter 34.* (1989) London: The Stationery Office.

Great Britain. *Limitation Act 1980. Elizabeth II. Chapter 40.* (1980) London: The Stationery Office.

Great Britain. *Limited Liability Partnerships Act 2000. Elizabeth II. Chapter 12.* (2000) London: The Stationery Office.

Great Britain. *Limited Liability Partnerships Act (Northern Ireland) 2002. Elizabeth II. Chapter 12.* (2002) London: The Stationery Office.

Great Britain. *Misrepresentation Act 1967. Elizabeth II. Chapter 7.* (1967) London: The Stationery Office.

Great Britain. *National Minimum Wage Act 1998. Elizabeth II. Chapter 39* (1998) London: The Stationery Office.

Great Britain. *Occupiers' Liability Act 1957. Elizabeth II. Chapter 31.* (1957) London: The Stationery Office.

Great Britain. *Offices, Shops and Railway Premises Act 1963. Elizabeth II. Chapter 41.* (1963) London: The Stationery Office.

Great Britain. *Road Traffic Act 1982. Elizabeth II. Chapter 20.* (1982) London: The Stationery Office.

Great Britain. *Sale of Goods Act 1979. Elizabeth II. Chapter 54.* (1979) London: The Stationery Office.

Great Britain. *Sale of Goods (Amendment) Act 1994. Elizabeth II. Chapter 32.* (1994) London: The Stationery Office.

Great Britain. *Supply of Goods and Services Act 1982. Elizabeth II. Chapter 29.* (1982) London: The Stationery Office.

Great Britain. *Unfair Contract Terms Act 1977. Elizabeth II. Chapter 50.* (1977) London: The Stationery Office.

Great Britain. *Unsolicited Goods and Services Act 1971. Elizabeth II. Chapter 30.* (1971) London: The Stationery Office.

Treaty establishing the European Economic Community, Rome, 25 March 1957: text in force on 1 January 1973. London: HMSO.

3 Edw. I, c. 15 *(Statute of Westminster I 1275)*.

7 Edw. VII, c. 24 *(Limited Partnerships Act 1907)*.

42 Geo. III, c. 73 *(Factory Act 1802)*.

36 & 37 Vict., c. 66 *(Supreme Court of Judicature Act 1873)*.

38 & 39 Vict., c. 77 *(Supreme Court of Judicature Act 1875)*.

53 & 54 Vict., c. 39 *(Partnership Act 1890)*.

3 & 4 Will. IV, c. 103 *(Factory Act 1833)*.

Table of statutory instruments

Electronic Commerce (EC Directive) Regulations 2002 (SI 2002/2013).

Sale and Supply of Goods to Consumers Regulations 2002 (SI 2002/3045).

Unfair Terms in Consumer Contracts Regulations 1999 (SI 1999/2083).

Working Time Regulations 1998 (SI 1998/1833).

Table of cases

Adams v Cape Industries plc [1990] Ch 433.

Adams v Lindsell (1818) 1 B & Aid 680.

Alcock v Chief Constable of South Yorkshire [1991] 1 AC 310.

Allen v Flood and Taylor [1898] AC 1.

Allen v Gold Reefs of West Africa Ltd [1900] 1 Ch 656.

Anglia Television v Reed [1972] 1 QB 60.

Anns v Merton London Borough Council [1978] AC 728.

Aparau v Iceland Frozen Foods plc (No. 2) [2000] ICR 341.

Bannerman v White (1861) 4 LT 740.

Barber v Somerset County Council [2004] IRLR 475.

Beattie v E. & F. Beattie Ltd [1938] Ch 708.

Bettini v Gye (1875–76) LR 1 QBD 183.

Bolton v Stone [1951] AC 580.

Brown v British Abrasive Wheel Co [1919] 1 Ch 290.

Bushell v Faith [1970] AC 1099.

Candler v Crane Christmas & Co [1951] 2 KB 164.

Caparo Industries plc v Dickman and Others [1990] 2 AC 605.

Carlill v Carbolic Smoke Ball Co [1893] 1 QB 256.

Carmichael v National Power plc [1999] 1 WLR 2042.

Cassidy v Ministry of Health [1951] 2 KB 343.

Central London Property Trust Ltd v High Trees House Ltd [1947] 1 KB 130.

Currie v Misa (1875) LR 10 Ex 153.

Curtis v Chemical Cleaning & Dyeing Co [1951] 1 KB 805.

D. & C. Builders v Rees [1966] 2 QB 617.

Daimler Co Ltd v Continental Tyre & Rubber Co (Great Britain) Ltd [1916] 2 AC 307.

Davis v Johnson [1979] AC 264.

Devis (W.) & Sons Ltd v Atkins [1977] AC 931.

DHN Food Distributors v London Borough of Tower Hamlets [1976] 1 WLR 852.

Dickinson v Dodds (1875–76) LR 2 ChD 463.

Donoghue v Stevenson [1932] AC 562.

Dorchester Finance Co Ltd v Stebbing [1989] BCLC 498.

Eley v Positive Government Security Life Assurance Co Ltd (1876) 1 ExD 88.

Entores v Miles Far Eastern Corporation [1955] 3 WLR 48.

Felthouse v Brindley (1862) 6 LT 157.

Fibrosa Spolka Akcyjna v Fairbairn Lawson Coombe Barbour Ltd [1943] AC 32.

Foakes v Beer (1883–4) LR 9 App Cas 605.

Foss v Harbottle 67 ER 189.

Freeman & Lockyer v Buckhurst Properties (Mangal) Ltd [1964] 2 QB 480.

Froom v Butcher [1976] 2 QB 286.

Gilford Motor Co v Horne [1933] Ch 935.

Great Northern Railway Co v Swaffield (1873–74) LR 9 Ex 132.

Greenhalgh v Arderne Cinemas Ltd [1951] Ch 286.

Hadley v Baxendale (1854) 9 Ex 341.

Harris v Nickerson (1873) LR 8 QB 286.

Harrods Ltd v R. Harrod Ltd (1923) 41 RPC 74.

Hartley v Ponsonby (1857) 7 El & Bl 872.

Hedley Byrne & Co Ltd v Heller & Partners Ltd [1964] AC 465.

Hely-Hutchinson v Brayhead Ltd [1968] 1 QB 549.

Hickman v Kent or Romney Sheepbreeders' Association [1915] 1 Ch 881.

Hivac v Park Royal Scientific Equipment [1946] Ch 169.

Hogg v Cramphorn [1967] Ch 254.

Holwell Securities v Hughes [1974] 1 WLR 155.

Hong Kong Fir Shipping Co Ltd v Kawaski Kisen Kaisha Ltd [1926] 2 QB 26.

Household Fire Insurance & Carriage Accident Insurance Co Ltd v Grant (1878–79) LR 4 ExD 216.

Hyde v Wrench (1840) 49 All ER Rep 132.

Illingworth v Houldsworth [1904] AC 355.

Interfoto Picture Library Ltd v Stiletto Visual Programmes Ltd [1989] QB 433.

J. Evans & Son (Portsmouth) Ltd v Andrea Merzario Ltd [1976] 2 All ER 930.

John Shaw and Sons (Salford), Ltd v Peter Shaw and John Shaw [1935] 2 KB 113.

Jones v Livox Quarries Ltd [1952] 2 QB 608.

Kelner v Baxter (1866–67) LR 2 CP 174.

Koufos v C. Czarnikow Ltd, The Heron II [1967] 3 WLR 1491.

L'Estrange v Graucob Ltd [1934] 2 KB 394.

Limpus v London General Omnibus Co (1862) 1 H&C 526.

Lister v Hesley Hall Ltd [2002] 1 AC 215.

London Assurance v Mansel (1879) LR 11 ChD 363.

Macaura v Northern Life Assurance [1925] AC 619.

Mahon v Osborne [1939] 2 KB 14.

Marc Rich & Co v Bishop Rock Marine Co Ltd [1996] AC 211.

Market Investigations Ltd v Minister of Social Security [1969] 2 QB 173.

Murphy v Brentwood District Council [1990] 1 AC 398.

Nethermere (St Neots) v Taverna and Gardiner [1984] ILRL 240.

New British Iron Co, Re, ex parte Beckwith [1898] 1 Ch 324.

O'Kelly v Trusthouse Forte plc [1983] 3 All ER 456.

Olley v Marlborough Court Ltd [1949] 1 KB 532.

Osman v UK [1999] 1 FLR 193.

Panorama Developments (Guildford) Ltd v Fidelis Furnishing Fabrics Ltd [1971] 2 QB 711.

Pender v Lushington (1877) 6 ChD 70.

Percival v Wright [1902] 2 Ch 421.

Pharmaceutical Society of Great Britain v Boots Cash Chemists [1953] 2 WLR 427.

Phonogram Ltd v Lane [1982] QB 938.

Pinnel's case (1602) 5 Co Rep 117a.

Polkey v A.E. Dayton Services Ltd [1988] ICR 142.

Pollock v Macrae 1922 SC (HL) 192.

Practice Statement (Judicial Precedent) [1966] 1 WLR 1234.

Rayfield v Hands [1958] 2 WLR 851.

Ready Mixed Concrete (South East) Ltd v Minister of Pensions and National Insurance [1968] 2 QB 497.

Re Bond Worth Ltd [1980] Ch 228.

Re H R Harmer Ltd [1959] 1 WLR 62.

Re Selectmove [1995] 1 WLR 474.

Re Yorkshire Woolcombers Ltd [1903] 2 Ch 284.

Robb v Green [1895] 2 QB 315.

R.W. Green Ltd v Cade Bros Farms [1978] 1 Lloyd's Rep 602.

Salomon v Salomon & Co Ltd [1897] AC 2.

Savoia v Chiltern Herb Farms Ltd [1981] 1 IRLR 65.

Scott Group v McFarlane [1978] 1 NZLR 553.

Secretary of State for Employment v ASLEF [1972] 2 QB 455.

Simmonds v Dowty Seals Ltd [1978] IRLR 211.

Singh v London Country Bus Services Ltd [1976] IRLR 176.

Smith v Leech Brain & Co [1962] 2 QB 405.

Southern Foundries (1926) Ltd and Federated Foundries Ltd v Shirlaw [1940] AC 701.

South Pacific Manufacturing Co Ltd v New Zealand Security Consultants & Investigations Ltd [1992] 2 NZLR 282.

Spring v Guardian Assurance [1995] 2 AC 296.

Stilk v Myrick (1809) 2 Camp 317; 6 Esp 129.

Summers v Solomon (1857) 7 El & Bl 879.

Taylor v Caldwell (1863) 3 Best and Smith 826.

The Moorcock [1886–1890] All ER Rep 530.

Thomas National Transport (Melbourne) Pty and Pay v May and Baker (Australia) Pty Ltd [1966] 2 Lloyd's Rep 347.

Thompson v London Midland & Scottish Railway Co [1929] All ER 474.

Thornton v Shoe Lane Parking Ltd [1971] 2 WLR 585.

Twycross v Grant 2 CPD 469.

Ultramares Corporation v Touche 255 NY 170, 174 NE 441

Universe Tankships of Monrovia v International Transport Workers Federation (The Universe Sentinel) [1982] 2 WLR 803.

Vaux and Associated Breweries v Ward (No. 2) (1970) 5 ITR 62.

Walker v Crystal Palace Football Club [1910] 1 KB 87.

Warner Bros v Nelson [1937] 1 KB 209.

White v Jones [1995] 1 All ER 691.

William Hill Organisation Ltd v Tucker [1998] IRLR 313.

Williams v Roffey Bros & Nicholls (Contractors) Ltd [1991] 1 QB 1.

Wilson v Jones (1867) LR 2 Exch 139.

With v O'Flanagan [1936] 1 All ER 727.

Woolfson v Strathclyde Regional Council 1978 SC (HL) 90.

Yewens v Noakes (1880) 6 QBD 530.

Books and other materials

Combined Code on Corporate Governance (2008), London, Financial Reporting Council.

Porter, B., Simon, J. and Hatherly, D. (2008) *Principles of External Auditing* (3rd edn), Chichester, John Wiley & Sons Ltd.

The UK Corporate Governance Code (2010), London, Financial Reporting Council.

Acknowledgements

Grateful acknowledgement is made to the following sources:

Cover image: © Pgiam/iStockphoto.com

Text

Page 17: Crown copyright material is reproduced under Class License Number C01W0000065 with the permission of the Controller of HMSO and the Queen's Printer for Scotland

Page 18: Council of the European Union

Page 22: Crown copyright material is reproduced under Class License Number C01W0000065 with the permission of the Controller of HMSO and the Queen's Printer for Scotland

Figure

Figure 1: UK court structure. Reproduced under the terms of the Click-Use Licence

Illustrations

Page 11: © Vahan Shirvanian, www.CartoonStock.com

Page 13: © Dave Carpenter, www.CartoonStock.com

Page 16: © Dave Carpenter, www.CartoonStock.com

Page 35: © Fran, www.CartoonStock.com

Page 42: Carbolic smoke ball (1893) newspaper advertisement. This image is in the public domain because its copyright has expired.

Page 44: © Mike Flanagan, www.CartoonStock.com

Page 45: © S. Harris, www.CartoonStock.com

Page 53: © Chris Wildt, www.CartoonStock.com

Page 57: © Nick Downes, www.CartoonStock.com

Page 59: © John Morris, www.CartoonStock.com

Page 71: © Roy Delgado, www.CartoonStock.com

Page 72: © Kes, www.CartoonStock.com

Page 73: © Dave Carpenter, www.CartoonStock.com

Page 74: © Hagen, www.CartoonStock.com

Page 75: © Eldon Pletcher, www.CartoonStock.com

Page 95: © Mike Mosedale, www.CartoonStock.com

Page 100: © Fran, www.CartoonStock.com

Page 115: © Mike Flanagan, www.CartoonStock.com

Every effort has been made to contact copyright holders. If any have been inadvertently overlooked the publishers will be pleased to make the necessary arrangements at the first opportunity.